WRAPPED IN GEMS

WRAPPED IN GEMS

40 elegant designs for wire-wrapped gemstone jewelry

MAI SATO-FLORES
WITH JESSE FLORES

POTTER CRAFT

NEW YORK

To our parents, Seiichi and Kikue Sato and Jesse and Elodia Flores,

who brought us up with a great appreciation of nature.

Copyright © 2008 by Mai Sato-Flores and Jesse Flores

All rights reserved.

Published in the United States by Potter Craft, an imprint of the Crown Publishing Group,
a division of Random House, Inc., New York.
www.pottercraft.com

POTTER CRAFT and colophon is a registered trademark of Random House, Inc.

Library of Congress Cataloging-in-Publication Data is available upon request.

ISBN: 978-0-307-40846-4
Printed in China

Design by La Tricia Watford
Photographs by Marcus Tullis
Illustrations by Frances Soohoo

10   9   8   7   6   5   4   3   2   1

First Edition

CONTENTS

INTRODUCTION

NATURE AS INSPIRATION

I believe that the beauty and the exquisiteness of the natural world provide the best inspiration and ideas for jewelry designs.

Nature's designs are available to everyone. You don't have to go out hiking to find the right inspiration. It's just outside your door or maybe even in flowerpots in your home. I find plenty of ideas from nature, even living in New York City, by just observing my surroundings carefully.

Take a look at a tree or a plant—the contours of its leaves might make a great shape for a pendant, and the combination of colors in the leaves or the flowers could inspire your choice of gemstones. Branches, twigs, patterns of leaf growth, or the shape of a tree or plant itself provide endless ideas for earrings, bracelets, necklaces, and rings.

Designs that are in harmony with nature provide a feeling of tranquility and quiet luxury. It is great advice to "stop and smell the flowers." But don't just smell them. Look closely at their designs, their shapes, their outlines, and their combinations of colors. Look at them from different angles. Look at their leaves, and look at the little bugs on them. They are all great design ideas that can be used to make beautiful jewelry. A visit to the produce section at your local market, a stroll through the park or a garden, or a visit to a flower shop can all provide you with great design ideas.

Many design patterns become popular for short periods, but the patterns and shapes that mimic nature have had longevity throughout history and among all cultures. Most of these shapes and patterns are repeated in nature on both large and small scales with symmetry, harmony, and balance.

This book is loaded with ideas for translating what you see in nature into beautiful jewelry designs using materials such as wire, chain, and beautiful gemstones. Gemstones have fascinated people for thousands of years as a result of their color, clarity, and overall brilliance. You will see many examples of how gemstones of rich and vibrant color can be used to represent the colors of fruits, flowers, creatures, and other natural creations in jewelry in the pages that follow.

The vibrant colors of fruit can be represented in an array of beautiful gems like those used for the Pear Blossom Earrings on page 61.

WHAT'S IN THIS BOOK?

A guide to gemstones defines what they are, how they are made, and the standards for judging them. I've also included a brief history of gemstones along with a list of important terms used to describe their features.

The "Gallery of Creations" (pages 27-79) features photographs of my jewelry designs. The gallery has four sections, each of which represents something in nature that inspired the jewelry designs. It also describes how gemstones and wire can represent the patterns and designs of nature and includes information about the kinds of gemstones used.

In Part Three, you'll find instructions on how to make the 40 elegant jewelry projects featured in the gallery. The projects are organized by level of difficulty (easy, intermediate, and advanced). The easiest are presented first, and the designs progress to more advanced projects from there. If you are familiar with wire techniques, skim through the easy projects to see if there is a design that piques your interest, or go right to the intermediate designs. Some of the intermediate projects incorporate many of the same techniques involved in the easy projects but may have more steps involved or they may require new techniques that you will be guided through. The advanced projects are great for experienced jewelry artisans or for beginners who have worked their way through the other projects in this book and mastered the techniques.

Finally, I've included a resource section that covers everything from tools and materials to basic wire techniques and information on shopping for your gemstones and other materials. The Basic Techniques section includes the skills you will need to make the most of the projects in the book.

The natural symmetry of flowers provides the perfect inspiration for the flower earrings on page 35.

A PERSONAL JOURNEY

My interest in jewelry began when I was about seven years old and began to make beaded pieces for my friends. When I turned 20, I moved to New York City and began taking jewelry-making classes. I took metalsmithing and pearl-stringing courses, but in my spare time I began to explore wire techniques. I found wire easy and fun to work with; it can be bent and twisted into all kinds of shapes and forms, and you can do just about anything with it without having to use many tools.

People often ask me how nature became such a significant part of my jewelry designs. I tell them that there was no plan or grand design. I grew up in Takasaki, Japan, a city surrounded by mountains famous for their many natural hot springs. My parents love the outdoors and raised my sister and me with plenty of outdoor activities. We spent a lot of time camping and fishing in the mountains near our home.

I guess I missed being close to nature when I moved to New York because I found that most of my jewelry designs were inspired by plants, creatures, and other forms from the natural world. I was also inspired by the beauty of nature that was all around me in the city. Even in a metropolis like New York City, I was surrounded by natural life. It is amazing what you find if you pay close attention to what is around. I often go out on what I call "urban nature safaris." Basically, I just go out for a walk to focus on any plant, tree, or natural life I might find. Nature is resilient. On my safaris, I see trees that grow through fences, bend steel, and break through concrete sidewalks in their effort to grow. I find tomato plants growing in the cracks of sidewalks and plants that grow between bricks on the sides of buildings. I discover strange and colorful fruits and berries and new plants and flowers in shapes that I've never seen before. I discover tiny fragrant flowers growing in the grass while I'm lying in Central Park getting some sun, and I've discovered that the city is filled with an amazing array of trees.

I was born and raised in Japan, and I have been influenced by Japanese design principles. Within the tradition of Zen Buddhism, beauty is that which is in perfect harmony with nature and has a tranquil effect upon the viewer. I seek to create this same effect with my jewelry.

I like to create pieces that are not perfectly symmetrical but still maintain balance. This is typical of the Wabi and Sabi elements as they relate to design in which things are made to appear as if they were made by nature itself. The design of Japanese Zen gardens is guided by the idea that the shapes and textures of all the materials should be harmonious.

Just as creating jewelry inspired by nature happened "naturally" for me, becoming a jewelry designer was also a natural process, not part of a master plan. My true passion is for making jewelry designs; I have so much fun doing it that I don't consider it work. I always carry a sketchbook with me so that when I get an idea for a design, I can draw it right away. I encourage you to do the same. I can't wait to get home to my materials to create the new design, and I often draft several versions of a piece before I get it just right.

At one point, I had made more jewelry than I could wear, give away, or sell to friends. I worked hard to refine my techniques and began to use higher quality materials in order to sell my work. After some time and a lot of persuasion from friends I finally agreed to try the street vending thing, and we set up "shop" on trendy Bedford Avenue in Brooklyn, New York. Soon, a local boutique owner asked whether she could sell my jewelry at her shop. I then tried street vending on 5th Avenue in Manhattan, and my designs had an even better reception there. The experience gave me a boost in confidence and helped me learn about people's jewelry preferences, but I knew the setup was only temporary.

Soon, a friend told me that a new jewelry boutique would be opening on Madison Avenue on Manhattan's posh Upper East Side, and that the shop owner was looking for local designers with one-of-a-kind jewelry who could bring in new designs frequently. I took the challenge and was selected as one of the boutique's featured designers.

Then, I heard about a new and unique initiative in New York's "NoHo" (north of Houston Street) neighborhood to promote designs and concepts by cutting-edge talent, and I learned that two showcases were becoming available. I eagerly submitted images of my jewelry, and was then informed that there were over 40 designers competing for the spaces. The next day I got a call from the management team asking me to come in with samples of my work. I was offered first choice, and now I have my own jewelry showcase a block north of SoHo, where I had always wanted to sell my work.

I'm not sure what the future holds, but I will continue to make jewelry as long as I'm having fun. Right now, I love making jewelry and am never short on inspiration from nature.

YOUR CREATIVE PATH

I hope that as you explore nature and the jewelry designs in this book, you will find great inspiration and ideas for your own designs. I also hope you will see how dynamic a medium wire is for creating unlimited designs, and that the earth's gemstones provide unparalleled color and sparkle for these creations.

Inspiration literally means to "breathe in," and it involves the process of taking in everything around us. A heightened awareness of the senses can aid in a heightened perception of the natural world. Using your five senses to more fully absorb and "breathe in" the beauty of the natural world will help you unleash your creativity. Confidence, creativity, and skill level build upon one another in a circular fashion, just like the cycles of nature. I hope this book will inspire you in your creative process.

Mimic the movement of living creatures in jewelry designs like the "Bee Necklace" on page 51.

PART ONE

Collaboration of Art and Nature

The earth creates amazingly beautiful stones through natural processes, and humans transform them into gems to highlight their beauty. What follows is an introduction to the wonderful, dazzling world of gems.

CHAPTER ONE

GEMSTONES—EXPRESSIONS OF EARTH

I use gemstones as my preferred medium for jewelry designs because they are a high-quality natural substance of amazing beauty. They have an upscale look and feel that provides a sense of confidence to anyone who wears them. And in today's global market, many gemstones can be purchased at affordable prices from many sources.

My interest in gemstones began as a child. I can remember being outside and stopping whatever it was I was doing because a rock sparkling in the sunlight had captured my attention. I would pick it up and marvel at its composition. "Look at the cool rock I found!" I'd shout. All the kids would begin searching for more sparkly rocks. "This must be worth a million dollars! More than a million—a thousand!" (After all, we were just five years old.)

WHAT IS A GEM?

What is a gemstone, a precious gem, or a semiprecious gem? The classic definition of a gem or a gemstone is that it is a mineral that has been cut or polished to show its inner beauty, and as a rule it must be hard, rare, and beautiful.

This sounds easy enough, until we see that there are exceptions for just about every one of the characteristics used in this widely accepted definition. For example, not all gemstones are minerals. Some gems are organic, such as amber, bone, jet, pearl, and coral. These nonmineral gems were created by living organisms like mollusks, trees, or animals.

The next trait of a gem is that it has been cut or polished. However, many gemstones are appreciated in their natural form without being cut or polished, such as crystals.

Another defining attribute of a gem is its hardness, also described as durability. Again there are exceptions. Pearls, opals, and turquoise are all considered gems, though they are not hard, but soft, delicate materials.

Next, let's consider rarity. To be rare means that something is extremely uncommon or that it is found infrequently. If this were really the case, then the discovery of new mines of a particular gemstone that make it more plentiful would cause it to lose its status as a gem. But this is not the case, and many other factors such as marketing and demand are a big part of how value is assigned to stones defined as gems in the industry.

In his book, *Secrets of the Gem Trade*, Richard A. Wise says "[I]n the world of gemstones, if it is rare and beautiful and if demand is strong, it is precious." "Beauty," he says, "drives demand, rarity drives price." He goes on to differentiate between "actually rare" gems, which are found in small numbers, and "apparently rare" gems which describes gems that are numerous but for which there is a very high demand, and thus makes them difficult to find.

The last consideration in the definition of gems is beauty. Beauty was not always what determined a stone's value. Its association with symbols and supposed powers may have made it more valuable. Of course, people's definition of beauty varies from place to place and from culture to culture. We've all heard the saying that beauty is in the eye of the beholder, and this is true with gems.

The terms "precious" and "semiprecious" have been used to distinguish between what are deemed the most beautiful and valuable stones in the gemstone industry, and those that have been deemed of lesser value. The list of precious stones includes diamonds, rubies, sapphires, and emeralds. Somehow, these stones received the term precious and all other stones—no matter how beautiful, rare, and durable—were relegated to the semiprecious category.

Part of the reason for this is that for most of history, people were unfamiliar with the many mineral stones that exist in the same colors as the precious stones. Thus, any red gem was mistakenly called a ruby, blue gems were called sapphires, green gems were called emeralds, and clear gems were called diamonds.

There are so many other gems that are beautiful and at the same time much rarer than these stones. In addition, the list of stones defined as precious has changed and has included stones such as turquoise, star stones, and all forms of beryl. Because the list of so-called precious stones changes all the time and unscrupulous dealers can use these terms deceptively, the U.S. Federal Trade Commission has even considered making the term itself illegal.

Antoinette Matlins and A.C. Bonanno, in their book *Jewelry and Gems: The Buying Guide*, explain that "[t]he terms precious and semiprecious are discouraged today, since they can be misleading; rubies, sapphires, and emeralds are only 'precious' in rare quantities, and there are many 'semiprecious' gemstones today that are rarer and more valuable than so called precious gems."

So there we have the standards that define gems. They are full of exceptions that provide an indication of how complex the world of gems can be. Factors of gemology, geology, and the disciplines of marketing and even lexicology are all part of the world of gemstones. As for what qualifies a gem as precious, I suggest that you look at each stone for its individual beauty and distinct personality, and make your own decision based on what you like or consider beautiful.

COLORED GEMSTONES AND "THE FOUR C'S"

The Four C's of colored gems constitute a grading system for determining the value of individual stones. The Four C's are color, cut, clarity, and carat weight. When it comes to colored gems, all four qualities are important, but color is by far the most significant.

Colored gemstones are the focus of the projects in this book. The types of colored gemstones are almost unlimited, and new gems continue to be discovered. Today's market offers more choices than ever before, so it pays to have an understanding of what's available.

Diamonds, which can also be found in different colors, have their own grading system called "the Four C's for Diamonds," and it is quite different from, and should not be confused with "the Four C's for Colored Gems." Pearls are evaluated by six factors, which are listed on page 20.

COLOR

When you ask someone why he or she likes a particular gem, they will most likely say that he or she admires its color, as opposed to any other characteristic. In the gemstone industry, color is the most important feature by which value is determined.

Gems come in every color of the spectrum, but for a long time the gemstone industry promoted very few of them. From the big chain stores to the small private jewelers, the focus was on the most profitable "precious" gems. This focus also created a demand for stones that resembled the most valuable gems.

With the globalization of the gem business and more gems becoming available through the Internet, people are discovering gems in many colors that have not been promoted by the gemstone industry. But because there is such a great variety, color is the main feature that causes so much confusion and misidentification of stones, even among the professionals.

It is important to know the basic terms that the gemstone industry uses to describe color. Hue, intensity (saturation), and tone are referred to as the "three dimensions of color" that apply to viewing gems. Distribution and light are also important terms in assessing color.

"Hue" is a technical term that describes a precise or pure color. It refers to the color you immediately notice when first viewing a gem.

Intensity and saturation are used interchangeably, and they describe the brightness of a color, or how intense or concentrated it is. They describe the strength or purity of the hue.

Tone describes the lightness or darkness of a stone color. It describes how much black, white, gray, or brown is present in the gem.

Distribution describes the way color is distributed in the gem and whether that color appears evenly throughout the stone.

Light is not a quality of gems, but it is of utmost importance when viewing them. You cannot accurately see the color of a gem without proper light. The stones absorb and reflect light, so the light source you use to view them can have a big impact on their appearance and bring out different colors in particular gemstones. For example, alexandrite, a very rare stone, looks green in daylight, but looks red in evening or incandescent light.

Before the advent of electricity, daylight from the north at noon was known to be the best for evaluating colored gems. This is because the color in sunlight changes from sunrise to sunset. Today, special lightbulbs reproduce various types of daylight and produce light with different effects on color. The color of light they produce is called "color temperature," and it is measured in Kelvin units. The most important thing to be aware of is that light affects the color of gems, and it is always best to view and evaluate them with different light sources.

CUT

Cut refers to the shape, or design of a stone. Gems can be cut in the cabochon (a convex, unfaceted cut) or faceted into one of many styles. As mentioned earlier, many gemstones, like the diamond, were not highly valued until people created the technology to cut them. While color, clarity, and carat weight are aspects of the gem that nature creates, the cut is the one element of its beauty that humans influence. When comparing two gems of the same color, weight, and clarity, it is the better cut that will determine which gem is more valuable.

Uncut gems are called "rough," and the artisans who cut them are known as lapidaries. The lapidary's objective when cutting a stone is to bring out the gem's optical properties or inner beauty while maintaining the maximum carat weight. The cut chosen for a gem can affect the depth of its color and its brilliance. Brilliance is described as the amount of light that is reflected from the inside of the gem through the facets, as well as from the surface of the facets. Gems are also evaluated for proportion (the balance of the design) and the finish (the detail of the workmanship).

In today's gemstone market, gems in many shapes are available as beads with a hole drilled through them. The gems used for the jewelry in this book all have a hole drilled through them so that they can be strung on wire.

CLARITY

Clarity refers to how clear a gem is, or to the absence of internal inclusions or blemishes on the gem's surface. Inclusions are foreign bodies found within the stone. It is important to know the distinction between an inclusion and a flaw. An inclusion only becomes a flaw if its presence negatively affects the beauty or the durability of the gem. Inclusions can sometimes enhance the beauty and value of gems.

Rutile crystals within a gem can create the asterism, or star effect, found in beautiful star gems like the star sapphire. Inclusions cause the cat's eye effect known as chatoyancy. They create the honey effect found in hessonite garnet, or the iridescent effect found in labradorite, or the billowy glow of moonstones.

Inclusions can also help identify the type of gem and where it is from by the types of foreign bodies it contains.

One of the ways the 4 C's are applied differently to judge diamonds versus colored gems relates to clarity. Evaluating diamonds requires the use of a jewelers loupe, which provides a magnification level of 10x. Evaluating colored gems does not require any such magnification, just the use of the naked eye. "Eye-clean" is a term used to describe gems that have no visible inclusions.

Because inclusions are so common in some colored gems and rare in others, three categories were developed to describe the degree to which inclusions in certain gems are eye-visible. Aquamarine, topaz, and green tourmaline are Type I stones because they typically have few inclusions. Emeralds and watermelon tourmaline are Type III stones because they tend to have more inclusions. Type II stones are the most common, and include garnet, iolite, peridot, quartz, spinel, and some tourmalines. But each variety of gem has its own clarity standards.

CARAT/WEIGHT

Gemstones are measured and valued by their weight; the unit of measurement for weighing them is the carat. Pearls are measured differently, that process will described later in the book (see page 20). One carat equals approximately .02 grams. The reason gems are measured by weight and not by size is that two gemstones of the exact same size can have very different weights. This is a result of the difference in their density, or what is also called specific gravity. Some materials have a higher density, and are thus heavier than others.

The sizes and shapes of stones are measured and cited in millimeters. In addition to the understanding the standards associated with the 4 C's, it is helpful to know a little about "wearability" and to learn some of the terms used to describe the special optical effects in colored gemstones.

HARDNESS AND DURABILITY

A stone must be hard to qualify as a gem. Why is hardness important? Soft gems, no matter how beautiful, can easily become scratched and thus lose their luster. The harder the gem, the better choice it is for jewelry.

Hardness refers to a stone's resistance to scratching. The "Mohs scale" has become the standard for determining the hardness of gems. Named after Dr. Frederich Mohs, the mineralogist who created it, the scale consists of a ranking of ten sample minerals with increasing levels of hardness. Each is capable of scratching the preceding mineral and can be scratched by the subsequent one. It is important to note that the difference between the levels is not the same.

MOHS SCALE OF HARDNESS

1. Talc	5. Apatite	9. Corundum
2. Gypsum	6. Orthoclase	10. Diamond
3. Calcite	7. Quartz	
4. Fluorite	8. Topaz	

For example, a diamond—the hardest mineral of all at number ten—is 140 times harder than corundum, which is ranked at number nine, and is eight times harder than topaz, which ranks at number eight. Your fingernail is a two and a half on the Mohs scale, so you can scratch talc and gypsum, but not calcite, which will scratch your nail. Quartz, the most common mineral on earth, is a seven on the Mohs scale. And dust is actually made mostly of quartz, so wiping dust can scratch the polish on any gem that is below a number seven on the scale. That is one reason great care must be taken when cleaning jewelry.

Durability (also referred to as toughness) is different from hardness, and it refers to how well a gem wears. Some stones can be very hard but not very tough. Toughness in crystal structures is related to their "cleavage." Cleavage, in reference to gemstones, describes how the molecules bind to one another and how the stone will break. Crystal gemstones have cleavage planes, and if they are hit just right, they can break cleanly in two.

LUSTER

Luster describes how the surface of a gem reflects light or how it shines. There are two main types of luster: metallic and non-metallic. Metallic describes the luster of minerals such as gold and silver, or gems like pyrite. These stones are opaque, which means light cannot penetrate them. Nonmetallic luster is transparent or translucent. Transparent means that light can pass through the stone, allowing you to see through it. Translucent means that light can pass through the stone, but it becomes diffused, so you cannot see through the stone clearly.

There are several terms used to describe nonmetallic luster. "Adamantine" is a brilliant luster, like that of a diamond. A "greasy" luster appears as if it had a layer of grease or oil, like jade or lapis lazuli. A "resinous" luster resembles resin, like that of hessonite garnet. "Vitreous" is a glass-like luster, like that found in topaz and many other gems. "Waxy" describes a luster with a waxy look like that of carnelian or turquoise. Other terms used to describe luster include dull, pearly, silky, and velvety.

PEARLS

Pearls are very different from mineral gems. A pearl is an organic gem that is not hard. A pearl is produced by saltwater oysters or freshwater mollusks. These gems are formed when a foreign body such as a grain of sand enters the shell of an oyster or a mollusk. It becomes an irritant, and as a defense, the mollusk produces a substance called nacre which then coats the irritant. It continues to make layer upon layer of this substance, which is made of microscopic crystals, and eventually becomes a pearl. The thicker the nacre, the more valuable the pearl.

People discovered that they could implant the irritant, usually made of mother-of-pearl, into the oyster or mollusk to "help" nature create what are known as cultured pearls. Cultured pearls are much more common than natural pearls, and they are more affordable. Just as colored gems have the 4 Cs, pearls have six factors that are used to determine their beauty, quality, and value. These are color, luster, nacre thickness, size, shape, and texture.

COLOR

Pearls can occur naturally in many colors. Their color is evaluated by considering the body color and the overtone. Body color describes the basic color of the pearl, such as white, or black, etc. The overtone describes translucent colors that can appear over the body, which are sometimes described as the tint. For example, pearls may be white with a pinkish overtone.

LUSTER AND ORIENT

Luster, as with inorganic gems, describes the reflection of light off the surface. The orient describes the iridescent glow that pearls display. The orient is what gives a pearl its distinct character. Not all pearls display the orient. Luster and orient are some of the most important characteristics that determine a pearl's value.

NACRE THICKNESS

Nacre thickness is considered one of a pearl's most important factors because it determines how long a pearl will last, and it creates the iridescent rainbow effect that occurs when light shines on it.

SIZE

The size of a pearl is determined by measuring its diameter in millimeters. Because pearls are much lighter than inorganic mineral gemstones, the unit of measurement used to determine and cite their weight is a grain, which is $\frac{1}{4}$ carat, and a momme, which is 18.75 carats. Four grains will equal one carat. Basically, the larger the pearl, the rarer and more expensive it is. Pearls from different parts of the world grow to different sizes, so this is taken into consideration when determining their value. For example, akoya pearls rarely grow very large, but South Sea pearls or freshwater pearls can grow much larger.

SHAPE

Because pearls are an organic substance, they come in many different shapes. There are three main shapes of pearls: spherical or round shapes; symmetric shapes; and baroque shapes, which are irregular and asymmetric. The gem market tends to place higher value on the more symmetric and perfectly round shapes. Within the categories above are many other shapes, with names like buttons, drops, near-round, and semi-baroque.

TEXTURE

Texture describes the surface of the pearl, which is often described as its "skin." Texture is sometimes referred to as "cleanliness." Texture can be bumpy or it can be very smooth. The bumps can be described as blemishes. Usually, the fewer the blemishes a pearl has, or the cleaner its skin is, the higher its value.

As was apparent in the lack of absolutes in the definition of what constitutes a precious gem, we know that definitions often change, and the value of gems can change depending on the values and demands of the market. What is beautiful in one society, culture, or time period can be regarded very differently in another. This fluctuation also applies to pearls. The gem industry may value a perfectly round white pearl, but you may decide that you find more beauty and value in a baroque pearl that displays rainbows of color. The choice is yours and depends on your individual design sense.

INDIVIDUAL GEMSTONES

The following pages provide information about the gemstones used for the projects in this book. It includes the names of the stones, the colors in which they are found, their level of hardness on the Mohs scale, their luster and transparency, and information on properties associated with the stones. I have selected these gemstones because they are beautiful and can be found at most gem and beading stores or through online vendors. You may choose to use the rarer gems, but keep in mind that they are extremely expensive and often difficult to find.

POPULAR GEMSTONES

Amethyst: The name is derived from the ancient Greek word *amethustos*, meaning "not drunk." The Greeks believed amethysts guarded agaist drunkenness.

Color: Varies from a deep rich violet-purples to lighter shades of pink to shades of lilac and mauve. Amethyst can also be found in a green variety.

Hardness: 7

Luster: Vitreous

Transparency: Transparent

Gemstone Facts: February birthstone. Amethyst is the most valued stone of the quartz group of minerals. Some amethyst is heat-treated, which then produces citrine, the yellow-colored quartz gem.

Lore: Amethysts are said to alleviate headaches and improve concentration and have been used to treat various skin conditions.

Ametrine: Called ametrine because the stone contains elements of both amethyst and citrine.

Color: Violet to golden

Hardness: 7

Luster: Vitreous

Transparency: Translucent to opaque

Gemstone Facts: Ametrine is among the quartz group of gemstones. It is found in stones that occur naturally with both amethyst and citrine crystals.

Lore: Ametrine is said to have a soothing effect on the soul, encourage creativity, symbolize growth, and promote a more mature and confident view of life.

Aquamarine: The name means "sea water" in Latin.

Color: Aquamarine varies from a rich translucent sky blue to a sea green. Dark blue stones are the most desired.

Hardness: 7½ to 8

Luster: Vitreous

Transparency: Transparent to opaque

Gemstone Facts: March Birthstone. Aquamarine is part of the beryl group of gemstone, which includes emeralds and morganite. Lighter blue stones are often heated to a darker blue.

Lore: It was believed that by turning darker or lighter aquamarine indicated what was true (dark) and false (light). It is also believed to be helpful for neck and throat problems and is thought to protect against colds and allergies.

Aventurine: It is named after a type of glass found in Italy that resembles green aventurine.

Color: Green, reddish brown, and golden brown

Hardness: 7

Luster: Vitreous

Transparency: Translucent to opaque

Gemstone Facts: Aventurine is a type of quartz and should not be confused with a stone called aventurine feldspar, which is also known as sunstone.

Lore: It is said to enhance a person's sense of humor and cheerfulness, and to stimulate dreaming. It is described as ideal for someone who is looking for a positive view of life.

Carnelian: Because of its similar color, carnelian is named after the kornel cherry.

Color: Brownish red to orange

Hardness: 7

Luster: Vitreous to waxy

Transparency: Translucent to dull

Gemstone Facts: Carnelian is part of the chalcedony group of stones. The Egyptians, Greeks, and Romans carved carnelian into many shapes for rings, cameos, and intaglios.

Lore: It is said to be effective in the treatment of blood disorders. Carnelian also symbolizes activity and is said to encourage community spirit.

Citrine: Citrine's name is derived from the Latin word *citrus*, which means lemon, because of its lemony yellow color.

Color: Varies from lemon yellow to brownish honey-yellow or gold.

Hardness: 7

Luster: Vitreous

Transparency: Transparent

Gemstone Facts: Citrine is known as the stone of light, sun, and life. It is a variety of quartz that is rare in its natural form. Most citrine on the market is amethyst that has been heat treated.

Lore: Citrine is said to be beneficial to the nervous system, as it combats stress and depression. It is also believed to have a positive influence on the metabolism and immune system.

Freshwater Pearls: Freshwater pearls are a type pearl that comes from freshwater mussels.

Color: White, silvery white, pink, salmon, red, copper, bronze, brown, lavender, purple, green, blue, cream, and yellow

Hardness: 3 to 4½

Luster: Pearly

Transparency: Translucent to opaque

Gemstone Facts: Pearls are organic gems because they are produced by a biological process. Freshwater pearls form in mussels and clams that live in lakes or rivers, and are often found in irregular (baroque) shapes. Pearls can be dyed.

Lore: Pearls are said to promote wisdom and contentment. They are believed to alleviate or cure chronic headaches if worn directly on the skin, and they are thought to reduce allergies.

Green Onyx: This gem is a variety of chalcedony and is also called chrysoprase.

Color: Green to apple green

Hardness: 6½ to 7

Luster: Vitreous to waxy

Transparency: Translucent to opaque

Gemstone Facts: It is the most valued of the chalcedony group of stones, which includes carnelian, agate, onyx, and sardonyx. It was used by the Greeks and the Romans to make cameos and intaglios.

Lore: It is said to have a calming effect and to lead people to new intellectual attitudes. It has been used to combat high blood pressure and hardening of the arteries.

Hessonite Garnet: It is also known as "cinnamon stone."

Color: Ranges from yellow to orange to reddish brown, and can have inclusions that give it a honey-like appearance

Hardness: 7

Luster: Vitreous to resinous

Transparency: Transparent to translucent

Gemstone Facts: Hessonite garnet is part of the grossular series of stones in the garnet group. The Greeks and the Romans used hessonite garnet to carve cameos and intaglios.

Lore: The garnet group of stones is said to encourage feelings of joy, stimulate the imagination, and boost one's sexuality.

Iolite: This stone gets its name from the Greek word for violet, *iolite*. It is also called cordierite or dichroite.

Color: Iolite is found in violet, blue, and gray. The color of the stone changes depending on the angle from which it is viewed. This feature is described as "pleochroism."

Hardness: 7

Luster: Vitreous

Transparency: Transparent to translucent

Gemstone Facts: Iolite is sometimes called "water sapphire" because of its beautiful blue color. Although iolite is a hard stone, it can be brittle and is not a good choice for use in a ring.

Lore: Iolite is said to reduce anxiety and stress. It has been used to treat a variety of digestive problems and to reduce blood pressure.

Labradorite: It is named after the Canadian peninsula of Labrador, where it was first found.

Color: Dark smoke-gray base, but iridescent as moved. Can display rainbow colors of violet, blue, green, orange and yellow. This effect is called "schiller" or "labradoresence." It is caused by interference of light by distortions inside the stone.

Hardness: 6 to 6½

Luster: Vitreous

Transparency: Transparent to opaque

Gemstone Facts: Labradorite is part of the feldspar group of stones, which includes moonstone.

Lore: It is said to have a calming, harmonizing effect that helps clarify one's views. It is used to alleviate bone and joint problems, such as rheumatism and arthritis.

Moonstone: Moonstone gets its name from its opalescent moonlike appearance.

Color: Ranges from gray, brown, pink, yellow, green, peach, and the rainbow moonstone which varies from colorless to milky white with a blue to silver or yellow sheen when viewed at different angles

Hardness: 6 to 6½

Luster: Vitreous

Transparency: Translucent to opaque

Gemstone Facts: Moonstone is part of the feldspar group which includes, labradorite.

Lore: Moonstone is said to be the stone of love and lovers. It is said to stimulate love and sensitivity, encourage a youthful attitude, and bring inner harmony. It is believed to promote a natural hormonal balance and fertility in women and ensure easy pregnancy and delivery.

Peridot: The name peridot is believed to come from the Arabic word for gem, *faridat*. Peridot is also known as chrysolite or olivine.

Color: Varies from an olive or bottle green to a yellowish green

Hardness: 6½ to 7

Luster: Vitreous to oily

Transparency: Transparent

Gemstone Facts: Peridot is the August birthstone. It is often found in volcanic lava and has also been found in lunar rocks and meteorites.

Lore: Peridot is thought to combat envy and resentment and transform negative feelings into positive ones. It is said to improve the immune system.

Prehnite: This stone was named for its discoverer, Colonel Hendrik von Prehn.

Color: Pale to mid-green, yellow, tan, gray and white

Hardness: 6 to 6½

Luster: Vitreous

Transparency: Transparent to translucent

Gemstone Facts: Some prehnite can exhibit the cats-eye effect. It is often found in volcanic rocks.

Lore: Prehnite is said to bring inner guidance and a peaceful outlook.

Pyrope Garnet: Pyrope garnet is also known as Bohemian garnet.

Color: Red with a brown tint

Hardness: 7 to 7½

Luster: Vitreous

Transparency: Transparent to opaque

Gemstone Facts: Garnet is popularly known for the red pyrope and almandite species.

Lore: Garnet group stones are said to strengthen the heart and improve circulation. They are said to encourage feelings of joy, stimulate the imagination, and are believed to boost sexuality.

Rhodolite Garnet: The name garnet is derived from the Latin word for grain *granulum* because of its similarity to the red "grains" or seeds from the pomegranate.

Color: Purplish reds to rose hues

Hardness: 7 to 7½

Luster: Vitreous

Transparency: Transparent to opaque

Gemstone Facts: There are 15 different garnet species whose colors range from red to orange, brown, golden, yellow, and green.

Lore: Garnets are said to strengthen the heart and improve circulation. They are also said to encourage feelings of joy, stimulate the imagination, and boost sexuality.

Rose Quartz: It is named for its rosy color.

Color: Pale, strong pinks and peaches

Hardness: 7

Luster: Vitreous

Transparency: Translucent and semitransparent

Gemstone Facts: Rose quartz can have a crackled and cloudy appearance.

Lore: Rose quartz is said to have a beneficial effect on the heart and circulation and to combat love sickness. It is said to symbolize trust and has been used as a love charm.

Ruby: The name originates from the Latin word *rubeus*, which means red.

Color: Varying shades of red

Hardness: 9

Luster: Vitreous

Transparency: Transparent to opaque

Gemstone Facts: Rubies, like sapphires, are part of the corundum species. After diamonds, they are the hardest substance on earth. Rubies from Myanmar (Burma) are considered the finest.

Lore: Rubies are said to embody divine love in crystal form. Like other red stones, they said to strengthen the heart and circulation. They are also said to promote sexual energy. A ruby symbolizes love and passion.

Rutilated quartz: This gem gets its name from the needles of rutile quartz crystal enclosed within it.

Color: Golden to reddish, or even black with a metallic luster, but usually colorless

Hardness: 7

Luster: Vitreous

Transparency: Transparent to translucent

Gemstone Facts: The stone is also referred to as "the hair of Venus."

Lore: It is said to contain the light of the sun and to symbolize truth.

Sapphire: Sapphires get their name from the Latin word *sapphirus*, the Greek word for blue.

Color: Colorless, pink, orange, yellow, green, blue, purple, and black

Hardness: 9

Luster: Vitreous

Transparency: Transparent to opaque

Gemstone Facts: Sapphires are part of the corundum species. At first, only the blue variety of corundum was called sapphire, but today all colors of corundum go by this name, along with their identifying color, except the red corundum, which is called ruby, and the very rare pinkish-orange stone, which is called padparadscha. Next to diamonds, corundum is the hardest material on earth.

Lore: It is said to provide healing to the nervous system and to strengthen one's willpower. It is also said to symbolize faith, loyalty and friendship.

Smoky Quartz: It is named for its smoky color.

Color: Varies from light brown to gray to nearly black

Hardness: 7

Luster: Vitreous

Transparency: Transparent to translucent

Gemstone Facts: Gems called smoky topaz are usually not topaz but rather smoky quartz, and should be recognized as such. Rock crystal, also a member of the quartz group, can be heat treated to make smoky quartz.

Lore: In antiquity, soldiers wore it for protection, and it was said to warn of danger by turning darker. It is said to bring an inner calm, renew strength, and overcome grief.

Spinel: The name spinel is said to originate either from the Greek word *spinther* for "sparkling," or from the Latin word *spina*, for "thorn."

Color: Spinel can be pink, red, orange, yellow, green, blue, or black.

Hardness: 8

Luster: Vitreous

Transparency: Transparent to opaque

Gemstone Facts: People often confuse spinel gems with rubies or sapphires. Many famous gems that were thought to be rubies were later discovered to be spinel.

Lore: Spinel is said to speed the recovery of all diseases related to movement in the bones, joints, and muscles. It is described as a calming stone that reduces anxiety.

Topaz: Some sources say the name comes from the Sanscrit word *tapas*, which means "fire." Others claim it originates from the Arabic word *topazos*, which means "found." Still others say its name comes from an island off the coast of Egypt formerly known as Topazios, which was actually known for its peridot gems.

Color: Can be colorless, yellow, pink, blue, brown, or the golden color known as "sherry topaz"

Hardness: 8

Luster: Vitreous

Transparency: Transparent and translucent

Gemstone Facts: Topaz stones are often heat-treated to enhance color. Yellow stones are heated to make the rarer pink stones, and colorless stones are heated to make the blue stones.

Lore: Topaz is said to symbolize the joy of life, and is believed to ease tension. Yellow topaz is also said to counteract moodiness caused by lack of sleep.

Tourmaline: The name comes from the Sinhalese word *tourmali*, which means "stone with mixed colors."

Color: Tourmaline is found in pink, violet red, yellowish brown, various shades of greens and blues, and even black or a rare colorless form. Watermelon tourmaline is red inside and green outside.

Hardness: 7 to 7½

Luster: Vitreous

Transparency: Transparent to opaque

Gemstone Facts: There are 11 species in the tourmaline group of stones.

Lore: Tourmaline is known to symbolize friendship and love. Green tourmaline is said to strengthen the heart and nervous system. Blue tourmaline promotes detoxification of the body. Watermelon tourmaline alleviates pain and strengthens the immune system. Pink and red tourmaline detoxify the body.

Gallery of Creations

The shapes, patterns, and forms found in nature have a universal appeal. They have a rhythm, balance, and organic beauty that impart a soothing, tranquil effect. Jewelry designs that incorporate some of the harmony of natural shapes and forms can echo this effect. In this gallery, gemstones are combined with wire and chain to create elegant pieces that give a nod to Mother Nature's design sense.

CHAPTER TWO

BRANCHES AND BLOSSOMS

The natural designs of plants, leaves, flowers, and trees are all around us. Plant life grows in an abundance of beautiful and soothing shapes, colors, and forms. The bounty and the variation of our planet's plant life provide limitless ideas for jewelry design.

bouquet earrings

Sprays of color inspired by the blooms of Spring *(page 82)*

flower petal ring

The weighty quality of primrose petals in hessonite *(page 84)*

tiny twig earrings

Rhodolite garnet mimics buds that begin to blossom in organic shapes *(page 87)*

catkin earrings

The delicate ornaments of the willow

tree reflected in aventurine *(page 86)*

clover necklace

A collection of balanced clover leaves in tourmaline *(page 89)*

flower earrings

The dainty petals of a flower portrayed in peridot *(page 91)*

tree branch necklace

Smoky quartz gems provocatively balanced

in a natural asymmetry *(page 93)*

twig leaf earrings

Sprouting leaves on a twig soothingly depicted

in freshwater pearls with a smooth luster *(page 97)*

stem of leaves bracelet

Baroque freshwater pearls portray leaves in rainbows
of shimmering iridescent colors *(page 95)*

september leaves necklace

Unbalanced harmony represented with hues of
tourmaline to match leaves of early autumn *(page 98)*

sprouting sprig necklace

Nature's playful colors and shapes in
golden citrine and green peridot *(page 100)*

wisteria earrings

Cascading flower clusters in soft

shades of pink and lilac *(page 102)*

CHAPTER THREE

CREATURES OF THE EARTH

When you describe the variety of creatures on this planet, it sounds like something from a science fiction or children's fantasy book. There are creatures with one horn, two horns, giant antlers, and antennae. There are those with two legs, four legs, six legs, centipedes with one hundred legs, and creatures with no legs. From the tiniest one-celled creatures to giant whales, animals have so much beauty, balance, and symmetry, which, along with their colors and patterns can awaken your creative abilities and inspire unlimited ideas for jewelry designs.

baby octopus necklace

A transparent sea creature depicted

in bright and cheerful, translucent citrine *(page 105)*

bird motif earrings

Dangling tourmaline gems and distinctive golden
chain links create movement and sparkle *(page 106)*

jellyfish earrings

Translucent and prismatic gems reproduce the

ethereal and tranquil qualities of the jellyfish *(page 107)*

peacock feather earrings

Lengths of chain and rutilated quartz re-create

the pattern of a peacock feather *(page 108)*

butterfly necklace

Two separate chain links and amethyst gems

re-create the symmetry of a butterfly *(page 109)*

bee necklace

A bee with wings in motion as it hovers over a violet flower *(page 110)*

firefly necklace

Sterling silver and rainbow moonstone
express the flickering light of a firefly (page 113)

NATURE'S BOUNTY

Fruits are the means by which flowering plants spread their seeds. These seed containers are not only delicious but also pleasing to the eye in an array of beautiful shapes, designs, and bright colors, providing many ideas for jewelry designs and creations. When we think of life's indulgences or of celebrations, we think of food. It is part of our customs, ceremonies, and religious rituals. Why not celebrate nature's beautiful and delicious gifts with jewelry?

cluster berries earrings

Refreshing colors of sparkling rondelle gems bear

likeness to sumptuous and lush berries *(page 116)*

grapevine necklace

Opaque green aquamarine gems hang

off the chain like grapes on a vine (page 117)

currant necklace

A gracefully balanced and elegant design of
dainty and delicate gems in bold ruby red *(page 118)*

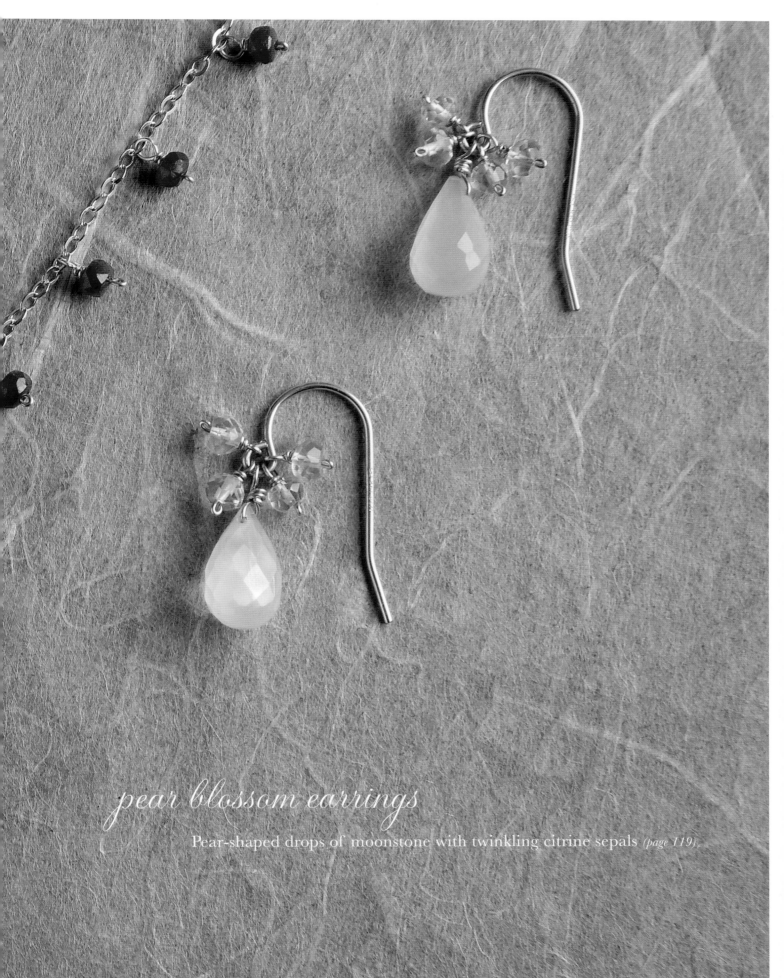

pear blossom earrings

Pear-shaped drops of moonstone with twinkling citrine sepals *(page 119)*

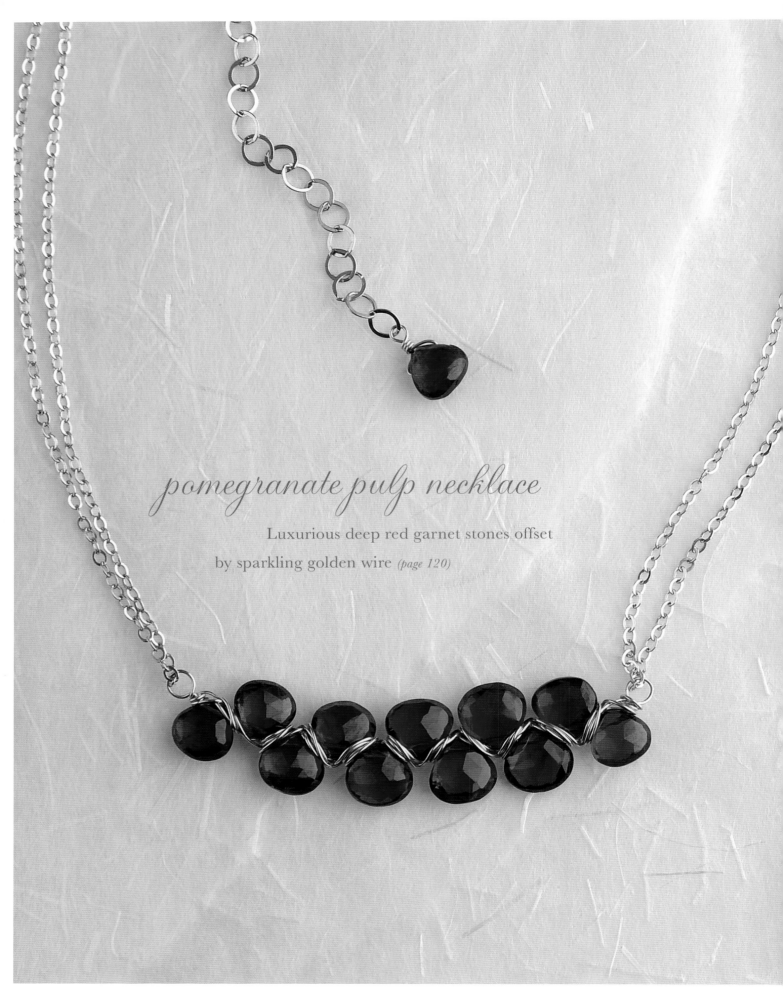

pomegranate pulp necklace

Luxurious deep red garnet stones offset
by sparkling golden wire *(page 120)*

orange pulp bracelet

Carnelian's waxy luster and cheerful

color replicates a juicy orange *(page 122)*

peas~in~a~pod bracelet

Soft green prehnite gems imitate peas in a pod *(page 124)*

summer peaches bracelet

Pleasing peach-colored moonstones and stylish flat,

round-link chain are the perfect summer adornment *(page 125)*

CHAPTER FIVE

EARTH AND SKY

The rivers and volcanoes, the raindrops from the clouds, and the moon and stars
exhibit their own unique fluidity and energy. In the shapes they take and the colors
they offer, we can find astounding inspiration. There is no limit to the things we
can find on the earth and in the sky to use as models for beautiful jewelry designs.

eclipse necklace

Sparkling amethyst gems re-create the glowing beams
of sunlight at the edges of a solar eclipse *(page 127)*

volcano earrings

Labradorite's rich play of iridescent colors represents the
volcanic earth, and golden chains look like flowing lava *(page 129)*

milky way bracelet

Rainbow moonstones exhibit the flashes of color in the night sky *(page 130)*

morning dew necklace

A sophisticated, well-balanced necklace with

gorgeous green amethyst gems *(page 131)*

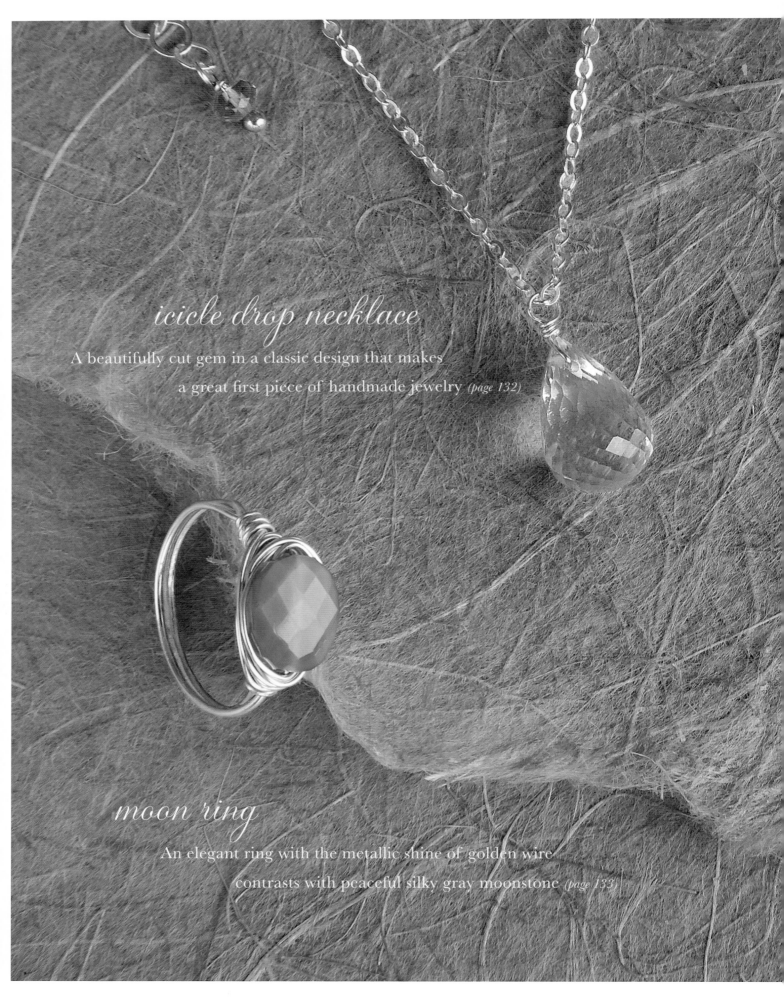

icicle drop necklace

A beautifully cut gem in a classic design that makes

a great first piece of handmade jewelry *(page 132)*

moon ring

An elegant ring with the metallic shine of golden wire

contrasts with peaceful silky gray moonstone *(page 133)*

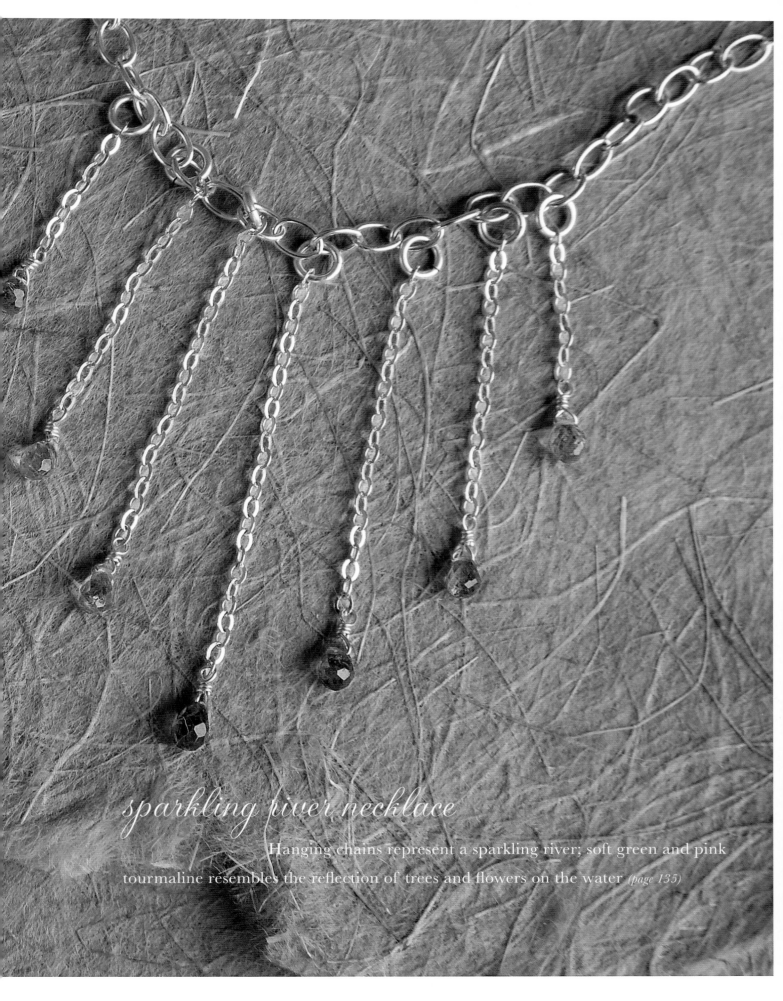

sparkling river necklace

Hanging chains represent a sparkling river; soft green and pink
tourmaline resembles the reflection of trees and flowers on the water *(page 135)*

ocean mist necklace

A necklace of refreshing drops of aquamarine

gems that can be wrapped around the neck twice *(page 136)*

saturn earrings

The soothing shape of circles

surrounding charming amethyst gems *(page 137)*

waterfall earrings

Silver flowing chains depict cascading
water; captivating green onyx portrays
a vibrant green pool *(page 138)*

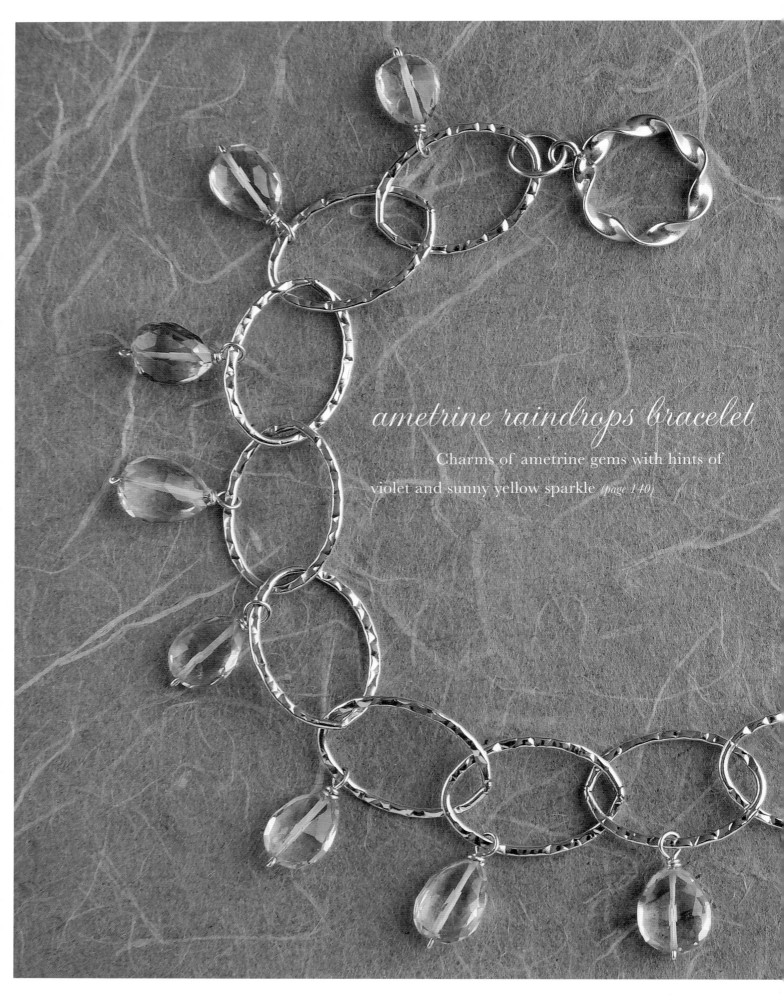

ametrine raindrops bracelet

Charms of ametrine gems with hints of
violet and sunny yellow sparkle *(page 140)*

stars of libra

Open chain links make beautifully balanced

earrings with alluring London blue topaz. *(page 139)*

shooting star necklace

A versatile lariat necklace with intriguing

misty gray and iridescent labradorite gems *(page 141)*

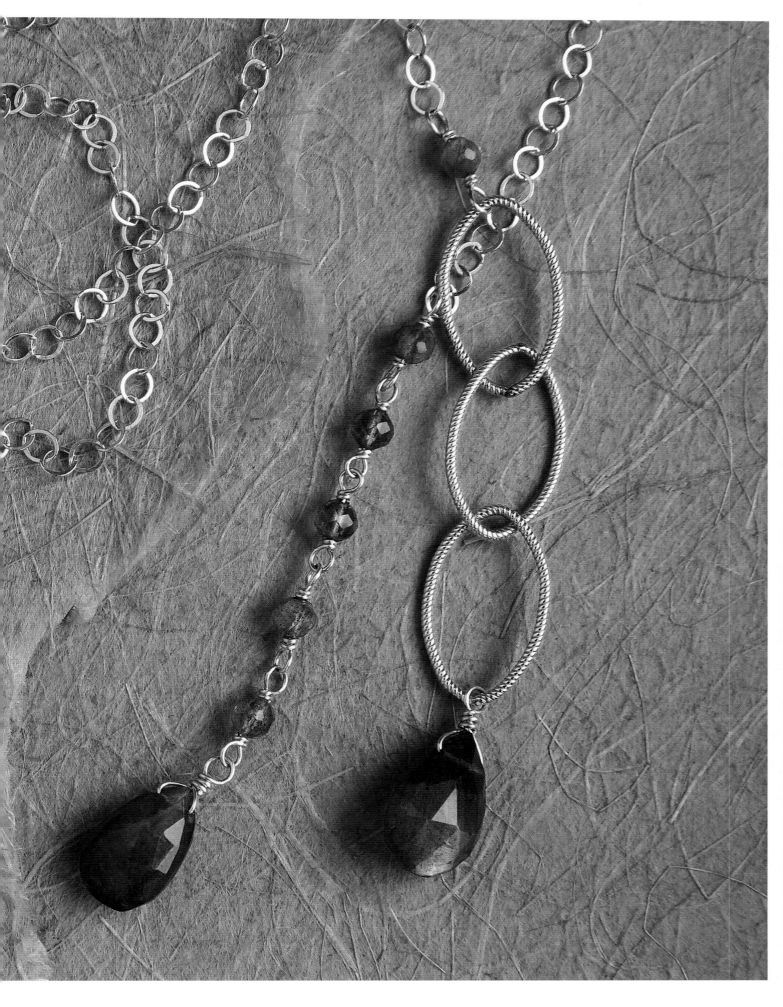

40 Elegant Designs for Wire~Wrapped Gemstone Jewelry

You've seen the gallery of creations inspired by the endless and magnificent designs of the natural world. Here are the design principles behind those creations, along with instructions for making them yourself using gorgeous gemstones, gleaming wire, and sparkling chains.

CHAPTER SIX

BRANCHES AND BLOSSOMS JEWELRY DESIGNS

A bouquet of flowers can lighten up a room with a sense of life, color, and joy. I've used colorful gems and golden wire to create earrings that can have that same bright and cheerful effect. Sapphire is an excellent choice to represent the flowers, since it is a bright, beautiful stone available in so many colors. The topaz in a light champagne color adds a transparent and sparkling luster that doesn't overpower the small sapphire gems.

LEVEL

Advanced

LENGTH

2⁵⁄₁₆" (5.9cm)

TOOLS

Ruler

Wire cutters

Chain-nose pliers

Flat-nose pliers

Round-nose pliers

MATERIALS

96" (244.8cm) of 26-gauge 14k gold-filled
   wire (soft)

Eighteen 9x6mm faceted, top-drilled,
   teardrop champagne topaz gems

Thirty 3mm faceted rondelle multicolored
   sapphire gems

Two 7mm 14k gold-filled jump rings

Two 14k gold-filled earwires

Note: Rondelle sapphire gems can be
purchased in strands with multicolored
gems. For this project, I've separated the
colors so that each depicts a different
color of flowers in a bouquet.

INSTRUCTIONS

1. Cut the 96" (244.8cm) of 26-gauge wire to 4 lengths that are each 6½" (16.6cm), and 8 lengths that are each 6" (15.3cm), and 4 lengths that are each 5½" (14cm).

2. Insert three 9 x 6mm top-drilled champagne topaz gems onto a 6½" (16.6cm) wire and slide them to the center of the wire.

3. Hold the center gem with your fingers, and pull the ends of the wire with your other hand until the gems make a clover shape. Cross the wires to form an X close to the gems.

4. Hold the three gems between your fingers and use the flat-nose pliers to twist the wire twice. Continue holding the three gems between your fingers and use your fingers from your other hand to keep twisting the wire until you reach the end of the wire. Then use the flat-nose or chain-nose pliers to twist the ends of the wire so that they are tight.

5. Repeat steps 2 through 4 twice, using the 6" (15.3cm) lengths of wire and 3 champagne topaz gems with each.

6. Repeat steps 2 through 4 using a 6½" (16.6cm) length of wire and three 3mm faceted rondelle sapphire gems of one color.

7. Repeat steps 2 through 4 twice, using the 6" (15.3cm) lengths of wire and three of one color of rondelle gems with each.

8. Repeat steps 2 through 4 twice, using the 5½" (14cm) lengths of wire and three of one color of rondelle gems with each.

9. Hold the 8 gem flowers and stems of twisted wire in one hand, with the three champagne topaz stems on the bottom and the rondelle sapphire stems on top, and make all the wire ends flush. Don't worry too much about positioning them now; you will be able to bend them into position later.

10. With the ends flush, hold all the gem flowers between your thumb and index finger and use your fingers from the other hand to twist all the wires together from the point where your fingers are holding the wires to the end of the wires.

11. Use the flat-nose or chain-nose pliers to twist the wires to make sure they are tightly wrapped and that no wires are sticking out.

12. Use the flat-nose or chain-nose pliers, and at 1½" (3.8cm) from the end of the wire stem, bend the stem to a right angle towards either the front or the back of the bouquet, but not towards the sides. (The champagne topaz gems are on the back and the rondelle sapphire gems are on the front.)

13. Use the round-nose pliers to make a wrapped loop with the bundle of stem wires, and then use the chain-nose pliers to press the wire against the stem. Then use the tip of the chain-nose pliers to compress the tips of the wire securely against the stem.

14. Adjust the stems so that the three champagne topaz gems are on the back and the colored rondelle gems are attractively positioned on the front.

15. Open a 7mm jump ring and insert the wrapped loop and the loop of the earwire. Close the jump ring.

16. Repeat steps 2 through 15 for the second earring.

FLOWER PETAL RING

I'm often struck with wonder when I look closely at a flower. It holds many parts and patterns that can be replicated in jewelry designs. You'll find flowers with three, four, or five petals, or two sets of three petals, or petals that spiral and swirl. They can have beautifully symmetric extensions from their centers. All these parts can be reproduced with gems and wire. This flower petal ring replicates a four-petal primrose. The hessonite garnet gems with their various shades of color, honey-like inclusions, and vitreous to resinous luster are entrancing stones that will catch the eyes of many admirers.

LEVEL
Advanced

SIZE
Flower—⅝" (1.6cm) diameter

TOOLS
Ruler

Wire cutters

Chain-nose pliers

Bent-nose pliers

Flat-nose pliers

Round-nose pliers

Ring Mandrel

Nylon, wooden, or rawhide mallet

MATERIALS
8" (20.4cm) of 20-gauge 14k gold-filled wire (soft)

13" (33cm) of 26-gauge 14k gold-filled wire (soft)

Four 7x7mm faceted, top-drilled teardrop shaped multi-colored hessonite garnet gems

INSTRUCTIONS

1. Use the wide part of the jaws of the round-nose pliers to hold the 8" (20.3cm) of 20-gauge wire at 3⅝" (9.3cm) from one end, then wrap the longer wire over the jaws and make a wrapped loop (page 152) that is about 3mm in diameter.

2. Hold the two wires together and straighten them so they are parallel, then wrap them around the mandrel at the size of ring that you want to make. Insert the ends of the wire into the loop, then hold the ring with your fingers making sure the wire is flush all around the mandrel as you pull the ends of the wire with the flat-nose pliers, then pull the wires back tightly to keep the shape and size you need. You can stretch the wire a bit later if you need to enlarge the ring, but you cannot make the ring size smaller.

3. Remove the ring from the mandrel and use the chain-nose pliers to wrap the parallel wires around the band of the ring next to the loop twice. Cut off any remaining wire and pinch the ends snugly to the band.

4. Reinsert the ring onto the mandrel and use the mallet to lightly tap the ring around the band, first tapping it perpendicular to the mandrel to give it a good round shape. Then tap it from the tapered side of the mandrel towards the wider side to make the wires of the band flush, or if you want to make it a little bigger.

5. To make the shape of the flower, insert the 4 multi-colored hessonite garnet gems onto the 13" (33cm) of 26-gauge wire so that they are adjacent to each other and about ½"(1.3cm) from the end of one side of the wire. Then, with your fingers on the wire next to the outer gems, gently bring the ends of the wires together until the gems form a circle (flower shape), and cross the wire into an X.

6. Hold the gems with one hand and use the flat-nose pliers to twist the wire above the X twice. Make sure the stones are evenly and loosely distributed on the stem wire before you twist the wire. Don't squeeze them too tightly against each other, as this can cause them to break, and you will need a tiny bit of space to wrap the wire in between the stones later.

7. Pull the two wires together so they are parallel and perpendicular to the flower, kind of like a flower stem, and then insert the wires into the open loop on the band of the ring. Center the gems so the center of the flower is directly above the center of the loop on the band, and hold them in this position with your fingers. Wrap the small wire over and around to the top of the flower, insert it into the center of the flower, and wrap it around the loop of the band in between two gems. You may need to use the chain-nose pliers or bent-nose pliers to pull the wire tight.

8. Keep holding the flower with your fingers on the ring as it is not stable yet. Wrap the long wire over and around the top of the flower, then insert it into the center of the flower. Wrap it around the loop of the band between two gems directly opposite from where you wrapped the small wire, and then use the tip of the chain-nose pliers to wrap the small wire around the band and make it snug.

9. Continue to fasten the flower petal gems to the band by wrapping the long wire over and into the center of the flower and around the loop of the band in between each of the gems once, moving in between each. Be sure to pull the wire tight so it is stable, but not extremely tight, as that can break the gems.

10. After you have made two full rounds wrapping the wire in between each of the gems, wrap the wire six times around the base of the four gems that form the flower to form a small bezel. Hold the wire down with your fingers as you wrap it because if you let go before you fasten it, it will become unwound.

11. To fasten the wire, insert it in between two gems and wrap it around the bezel wires three times. Use the tip of the chain-nose pliers to push the end of the wire in between the gems, and then pull it out on the other end. After you wrap it three times, cut off any remaining wire and make it snug.

CATKIN EARRINGS

In the springtime, trees like willow, birch, oak, and pecan grow long, cylindrical spikes of cascading tiny flower clusters called catkins. The green aventurine rondelle stones that appear to spiral around the chain, when hanging, represent these tiny falling flower clusters. This design also reproduces the rotational symmetry—the even balance visible all around an axis—found in nature.

LEVEL
Easy

LENGTH
2" (5.1cm)

TOOLS
Ruler
Wire cutters
Chain-nose pliers
Round-nose pliers

MATERIALS
3" (7.6cm) of 4x3mm 14k gold-filled flat
    cable chain (two 10-link lengths)
52½" (134cm) of 26 gauge 14k gold-filled
    wire (soft)
Forty-two 3mm faceted rondelle green
    aventurine gems
Two 14k gold-filled earwires

INSTRUCTIONS

1. Cut the 3" (7.6cm) of 4x3mm cable chain into two pieces that have 10 links each (1⅜" [3.5cm] each).

2. Cut the 26 gauge wire into 42 pieces that are each 1¼" (3.2cm), and make all of them into headpins.

3. Insert the 3mm green aventurine gems onto the headpins and then make an open loop (page 152) on 38 of them, and a closed wrapped loop (page 153) on 4 of them.

4. Attach one of the gems with an open loop onto the end link of one of the 10-link chains, then attach two gems to each of the remaining 9 links, attaching one on each side of the link, as shown in the photo, left.

5. Open an earwire loop and insert one of the gems with a closed wrapped loop, and the end of the chain with two gems on it (make sure one gem is on each side of the link you are attaching). Insert one more gem with a closed wrapped loop, and then close the earwire.

6. Repeat step 4 and 5 for the second earring.

The tiny buds that begin to blossom on the twigs of plants and trees are the first sign that spring will soon be sprung and that bare trees will soon be filled with bright colors. They are a sign of hope that says, "Soon we will be able to take off our heavy coats and once again spend days in the park or at outdoor cafés sipping tea with friends." These earrings celebrate the new life of spring with rhodolite garnet gems that represent the first buds, which often have a reddish color. These cute little sprouts on gold wire take the lovely organic shape of seedlings and newly sprung branches.

INSTRUCTIONS

1. Cut the 36" (91.6cm) of 26-gauge wire into two pieces that are each 18" (45.8cm) in length.

2. Insert a 3mm rhodolite garnet gem and slide it onto the center of one of the 18" (45.8cm) wires. Hold the gem with your fingers, and with your other hand, cross the wires over the point of the gem to form an X, leaving about 2mm of space between the gem and the X. Then, pinch the wire at the X and twist it twice; you could also use the tip of flat-nose pliers to twist it.

3. Insert 1 gem onto each of the two wires and slide them to the stem, hold the two gems between your fingers, and just as you did above, pinch the wire at the X and twist it twice.

4. Insert 2 gems onto each wire, and slide them to the stem, hold the two gems between your fingers, and just as you did above, pinch the wire at the X and twist three times.

5. Insert 1 gem onto one of the wires and hold the gem at ⅛" (3mm) away from the stem then tilt the gem so the wire bends to a right angle and pull the wire to the center of the stem so it makes the shape of a small triangle.

LEVEL
Advanced

LENGTH
1½" (3.8cm)

TOOLS
Ruler
Wire cutters
Chain-nose pliers
Flat-nose pliers
Round-nose pliers
Goggles

MATERIALS
36" (91.6cm) of 26-gauge 14k gold-filled wire (soft)
Thirty 3mm rondelle rhodolite garnet gems
Two 14k gold-filled earwires

6. Then hold the stem just above the gem between your thumb and index finger, and with the thumb and index finger from your other hand, hold the one gem on the triangle-shaped wire, pinch the tip of the triangle shape closest to the stem, and twist the wire gently three times. The reason you do not just hold and twist the gem is because the force of the wire twisting could cause the gem to break.

7. Twist the two stem wires once, repeat steps 5 and 6 on the opposite side, and then twist the stem wire 5 times.

8. Repeat steps 5 and 6, except this time use two gems and hold the gems at ¼" (6mm) away from the stem instead of ⅛" (3mm) as was done on step 5.

9. Twist the two stem wires once, then repeat step 8 on the opposite wire.

10. Twist the two stem wires six times.

11. Insert 1 gem onto each of the two wires and slide them to the stem, hold the two gems between your fingers, and pinch the wire at the X and twist it twice.

12. Use one wire to make a wrapped loop (page 152), but do not cut the remaining wire.

After you wrap the wire around the stem below the wrapped loop, wrap it over the two closest gems and around the stem below four times. Then, wrap the wire four times around the stem of the branch that holds two gems. Continue working your way down and wrap over the main stem four times, wrap over the stem of the next branch on the same side of the earring three times, then cross over the four gems to wrap the wire around the main stem twice. Wrap around the stem next to the last gem twice, cut off the remaining wire, and make it snug around the stem.

13. Repeat step 13 with the second wire, wrapping the wire around the twig branches on the opposite side of the earring.

14. Open the loop on an earwire and attach the wrapped loop, then close the earwire, and then shape the branches on the twig to a form you like. I like to put a slight bend on the twig so it has a natural and organic shape.

15. Repeat steps 2 though 15 for the second earring. If you made a slight bend in the shape of the first earring, make the direction of the bend of the second earring in the opposite direction so that when you wear them they both face the same direction. You can wear them with the bend facing forward, or alternate them so the bend faces back.

CLOVER NECKLACE

Clovers are delightfully attractive leaves that are evenly balanced with an odd number of smaller leaves. This design uses tourmaline gems with hints of brown, green, and yellow to represent the clovers. Once you learn the technique for making the clover design, you can use it in many other ways to make earrings, necklaces, bracelets, or pendants.

INSTRUCTIONS

1. Cut the 19" (48.3 cm) of 26-gauge wire to 7 pieces that are each 3¼" (8.3cm) in length, and one that is 1½" (3.8cm).

2. Making the clover shapes is similar to making a top-drilled gem loop (page 154) with 3 gems instead of one. Select three tourmaline gems in different shades, and string them closely together onto a 3¼" (8.3cm) wire, leaving one side of the wire longer than the other, approximately 2¼" (5.7cm). With your fingers holding the wire next to the outer gems, gently bring the wires together until the gems form the shape of a clover, and then cross the wire into an X, as shown in the photo left.

3. Use the tip of the flat-nose pliers to hold the wire above the X, and twist it twice. Cut the shorter wire and make it snug against the stem.

4. Use the long wire to make a wrapped loop, wrapping the wire around the stem three times, but this time do not cut the remaining wire. Wrap the wire diagonally between two gems once, then around the stem of the wrapped loop once, and then diagonally once again so you make an X shape over the gems. Finally, wrap the wire around the stem below the wrapped loop twice. Cut off any remaining wire and make it snug.

LEVEL
Intermediate

LENGTH
16" (40.7cm) to 18" (45.8cm)
(This necklace is adjustable.)

TOOLS
Ruler
Wire cutters
Chain-nose pliers
Flat-nose pliers
Round-nose pliers

MATERIALS
24¼" (61.7cm) of 26 gauge 14k gold-filled wire (soft)

Twenty-two 4x5mm faceted, teardrop, top-drilled multi-colored tourmaline gems

15" (38.1cm) of 5x2mm 14k gold-filled crinkle chain

2" (5cm) of 4x3mm 14k gold-filled cable chain

One 14k gold-filled lobster claw clasp

Seventeen 4mm 14k gold-filled jump rings

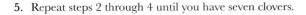

5. Repeat steps 2 through 4 until you have seven clovers.

6. Cut the 15" (38.1cm) of 5x2mm crinkle chain to 6 pieces that are each 1½" (3.8cm) in length, and 2 pieces that are each 1⅞" (4.8cm) in length. Use the technique on page 157 for cutting multiple chains of the same length.

7. Open a jump ring and insert the loop end of the lobster claw clasp, insert the last link of one of the 1⅞" (4.8cm) lengths of chain, and then close the jump ring.

8. Open another jump ring and insert it to the opposite end of the 1⅞" (4.8cm) chain, insert one of the clovers and the last link of one of the 1½" (3.8cm) lengths of chain, and then close the jump ring.

9. Repeat step 7 using the remaining 6 clovers and the 1½" (3.8cm) lengths of chain, then at the end of the sixth clover attach the 1⅞" (4.8cm) chain.

10. Open a jump ring and insert the last link of the crinkle chain and the 2" (5.1cm) 4x3mm cable chain, and then close the jump ring.

11. Use the 1½" (3.8cm) length of 26 gauge wire and the last gem and make a top-drilled gem loop (page 154) with an open loop and attach it to the end of the 4x3mm chain and close the loop.

FLOWER EARRINGS

While riding my bike in a park in Brooklyn in the springtime, I came upon a tree that had bunches of beautiful tiny green flowers with white centers. They were in a classic shape, kind of like something you would draw in elementary school, with five petals and the round center. The uncommon green petals inspired me to make these earrings. This design uses peridot gems and freshwater pearls to create classic flowers that hang on ball posts. You can easily attach them on long earring posts if you prefer.

INSTRUCTIONS

1. Cut the 14" (35.7cm) of 26-gauge wire into 2 pieces that are each 4" (10.2cm) in length, and 2 pieces that are 3" (7.6cm) in length.

2. Making the flower shape is similar to making a top-drilled gem loop (page 154) with 5 gems instead of one. Insert five peridot gems onto a 3" (7.6cm) wire and slide them close together, leaving one side of the wire longer than the other at approximately 1½" (3.8cm). With your fingers holding the wire next to the outer gems, gently bring the wires together until the gems form the shape of a flower, and then cross the wire into an X.

3. Use the tip of the flat-nose pliers to hold the wire above the X, twist it twice, and then cut the shorter wire and make it snug against the stem. Then, make a wrapped loop (page 152), and wrap the wire around the stem 3 times. Cut off any remaining wire, and make the wire snug against the stem.

4. Use a 4" (10.2cm) length of 26-gauge wire and insert the 3mm freshwater pearl to the center of the wire. Pull the ends of the wire so they are parallel to each other. Insert both ends of the wire into the center of the peridot flower petals, and pull them out on the other end until the pearl is flush against the center of the flower.

LEVEL
Intermediate

LENGTH
11/16" (1.7cm)

TOOLS
Ruler
Wire cutters
Chain-nose pliers
Flat-nose pliers
Round-nose pliers

MATERIALS
14" (35.7cm) of 26-gauge 14k gold-filled wire (soft)
Ten 5x4mm faceted, top-drilled, peridot gems
Two 3mm white, freshwater pearl gems
Two 14k gold-filled ball post with split loop earstuds

5. Wrap one of the wires from the pearl around and over to the top of the flower and insert it into the center of the flower in between petals 1 and 2, as shown in the photo, right, and pull it out of the bottom so it is wrapped around the wire holding the petals.

6. Use the wire from the other side of the pearl to do the same as in step 5, but wrap it in between flower petal numbers 4 and 5.

7. Then, proceed to wrap this same wire around the wire in between petal numbers 4 and 3, then finally between petal 5 and the wrapped loop.

8. Wrap the first wire used in step 5 in between flower petals 2 and 3, then between petal 1 and the wrapped loop.

9. Hold the two wires so they are parallel and wrap them together around the wrapped loop once, then cut off any remaining wire and make the ends of the wires snug to the stem.

10. Repeat steps 2 through 9 for the second earring.

Many designs in nature have natural asymmetry or unbalanced harmony, known as Fukinsei in Japanese, which gives designs a fresh and provocative look while maintaining balance. This necklace uses Fukinsei to be a bit playful, but the smoky quartz provides a mature and elegant counterbalance while the golden wire adds richness. Smoky quartz is a beautiful gem in a neutral color that matches well with almost all colors.

INSTRUCTIONS

Note: This necklace will be assembled in separate parts, including the stem of the branch segment on the chain and the stem of leaves pendant, which will all be joined to complete the necklace.

1. To make the branch segment on the chain, cut a 32" (81.3cm) length of 26-gauge wire and make a wrapped loop (page 152) at the center of the wire.

2. Insert a 9x7mm smoky quartz gem onto each of the wires and slide them to the wrapped loop. Then, hold the gems between your index finger and your thumb and cross the wires over each other to form an X with about 2mm of space between the gems and the X. Then, hold the wire at the X with the flat-nose pliers and twist it three times. Don't worry if the gems are little loose on the wires, you will wrap them with more wire later.

3. Repeat step 2 twice so you have 6 gems on the stem.

4. Insert another gem onto one of the wires and hold the gem at ¼" (6mm) away from the stem. Tilt the gem so the wire bends to a right angle and the sharp tip of the gem points toward the gems on the stem and pull the wire to the center of the stem so it makes the shape of a small triangle.

5. Hold the stem just above the six gems between your thumb and index finger, and with the thumb and index finger of your other hand, hold the one gem on the triangle-shaped wire and pinch the tip of the triangle shape closest to the stem and twist the wire gently three times. The reason you do not just hold and twist the gem is because the force of the wire twisting at the weakest part of the gem could cause it to break.

LEVEL
Advanced

LENGTH
16" (40.7cm) to 18" (45.8cm)
(This necklace is adjustable.)

TOOLS
Ruler
Wire cutters
Chain-nose pliers
Flat-nose pliers
Round-nose pliers
Goggles

MATERIALS
53¼" (135.3cm) of 26-gauge 14k gold-filled wire (soft)
Twenty-seven 9x7mm faceted, top-drilled, teardrop smoky quartz gems
17" (43.2cm) of 7x6mm 14k gold-filled flat cable chain
1³⁄₁₆" (3cm) of 4x3mm 14k gold-filled flat cable chain (9 links of chain)
One 14k gold-filled lobster claw clasp
Four 4mm 14k gold-filled jump rings

6. Repeat steps 4 and 5 on the opposite side, and then twist the two wires 5 times to extend the stem.

7. Repeat step 2 to add two more gems, and then make a wrapped loop with one of the wires, wrapping the wire around the loop 4 times, but do not cut the wire. You will use it to wrap around the stem and in between the gems.

8. Wrap one of the wires over and in between the first two gemstones once, and then wrap it in a coil around the stem about 9 times (the number of times you wrap may vary based on each individual piece). Then wrap the wire around the stem that extends out from the main stem several times. Wrap it back around the main stem a few times, cross the wire over and in between the next two gems once, and continue until you reach the point where you started. Now, wrap the wire around the stem next to the loop several times and then return wrapping it around the gems on the same side of the branch. When you wrap the wire to cross between the gems, wrap it so that it forms an X in between each pair of gems. When you run out of wire, bend the end so it is snug against the stem.

9. Use the other wire to do the same as step 8, wrapping it on the opposite side of the branch and crossing in between gems to form an X on the flip side.

10. Cut a 5¼" (13.3cm) length of the 7x6mm flat cable chain and then open a 4mm jump ring and attach the end link of the chain to the top wrapped loop of the gemstone branch you just made. Construction of the branch started on the bottom and ended at the top.

11. Cut an 11¼" length of the 7x6mm cable chain and open another jump ring and then attach the chain to the bottom-wrapped loop of the gemstone branch.

12. Cut the remainder of the 26-gauge wire into 17 pieces that are each 1½ " (3.8cm) in length, and use them to make a top-drilled gem loop (page 154) with an open loop (page 152) with each of the remaining 17 gems.

13. At the 5th link of the chain that is attached to the bottom of the gemstone branch, use a jump ring to attach the 1³⁄₁₆" (3cm) of 4x3mm cable chain, which should be 9 links long.

14. Attach and close one of the gems with an open loop to the bottom link of the 9-link chain. Then attach two of the gems with open loops to each of the remaining 8 links of this chain, attaching one gem on each side of each loop.

15. Starting with the link of chain that is holding the chain with gems that you've just completed, count to the 5th chain link in the direction opposite from the gemstone branch and attach a smoky quartz gem to this link. Do the same at the 7th, 9th, 11th, and 13th links.

16. Attach a gem to the wrapped loop at the bottom of the gemstone branch and at the first link of chain. This will create balance in the design.

17. Open a jump ring and insert an end link of the necklace and the loop of the lobster claw clasp and then close the jump ring.

18. Attach the remaining smoky quartz gem to the last link on the opposite end of the necklace.

STEM OF LEAVES BRACELET

Leaves are often thought of only in relation to trees and the seasons, but they are so much more. Like flowers, they grow in so many colors, shapes, and patterns. Baroque freshwater pearls can be found in the perfect shape to represent the leaf design. Many trees and plants grow their leaves in pairs that grow symmetrically and directly across from each other on the stems, while others grow in an alternate pattern on the stem. I use the baroque pearls to represent the leaves on a stem growing directly across from each other. The pearls provide a shimmering rainbow of iridescent colors that make this a radiant and enchanting bracelet.

INSTRUCTIONS

Note: This bracelet is made by joining three separate stem segments of pearls, which include one center segment and two small matching segments.

1. To make the larger center segment, cut a 36" (91.5cm) length of the 24 gauge wire, then bend a right angle at the center of the wire and make a Wrapped Loop (page 152).

2. Sort 18 baroque freshwater pearls by size, arrange them in the way they will be on the bracelet with two rows of 9 pearls that mirror each other and go from small on one end to large in the center, and then back to small at the other end.

3. Start with two pearls from one end and string one onto each of the wires. Slide them down to the wire-wrapped loop. Hold the pearls with your fingers and bend the wires across each other
to form an X, leaving about 2mm of space between the pearls and the X, and then hold the wire at the X with the flat-nose pliers and twist it twice.

4. Repeat step 3 eight more times using the pearls in the order arranged in step 2, and then make a wrapped loop, but do not cut off the remaining wire.

5. Use one of the two wires, and wrap it over and in between the first pair of pearls, then around the stem once. Then wrap over the next two pearls and around the stem once and continue until you reach the opposite end. Wrap it around the stem inside the wrapped loop once, then use the wire to return

LEVEL
Advanced

LENGTH
6" (15.3cm) to 7⅞" (20cm)

TOOLS
Ruler

Wire cutters

Chain-nose pliers

Flat-nose pliers

Round-nose pliers

Goggles

MATERIALS
81" (206cm) of 24-gauge sterling silver wire (soft)

18 baroque, flat, top-drilled, fresh-water pearls in sizes that range from 16x8mm to 21x10mm

Twelve 10x8mm (approximate size) baroque flat, top-drilled, freshwater pearls

1⅞" (5cm) of 4x3mm sterling silver flat cable chain

Four 4mm sterling silver jump rings (or more if you want to increase the length of bracelet)

One sterling silver toggle and bar clasp

wrapping the wire in between the pearls on the flip side of the stem until the wire ends, then make it snug around the stem.

6. Repeat step 5 with the second wire, wrapping the wire in the opposite direction so it forms an X shape in between each pair of pearls.

7. To make one of the smaller segments cut an 18" (45.8cm) length of the 24-gauge wire and bend a right angle at the center and make a wrapped loop, just as you did in Step 1.

8. Insert one of the 10x8mm baroque, flat, top-drilled freshwater pearls onto each of the two wires and slide them down to the wire wrapped loop. Hold the pearls with your fingers and bend the wires across each other to form an X, leaving about 2mm of space between the pearls and the X, and then hold the wire at the X with the flat-nose pliers and twist it twice.

9. Repeat step 8 twice, then make a wrapped loop, but do not cut the wire. Use it to wrap in between the pearls just as you did with the larger pearl segment.

10. Repeat steps 7 through 10 with the remaining 18" (45.8cm) length of 24-gauge wire to build the final pearl stem segment.

11. Open a 4mm jump ring and attach the end loop of one of the small stem segments to the larger center stem segment. Close the jump ring.

12. Use another jump ring to attach the remaining small stem segment to the opposite end of the larger center stem segment.

13. Open a 4mm jump ring and insert the wrapped loop of one of the small stem segments and loop of the toggle bar, then close the jump ring.

14. Open the last 4mm jump ring and insert the wrapped loop on the opposite end of the bracelet and the loop of the clasp, then close the jump ring.

TWIG LEAF EARRINGS

I got the inspiration for the twig and leaf design of these earrings on one of those perfect summer days in Central Park while lying in the shade under some trees and gazing upward. I watched the wind blow the leaves and sway the branches, and I listened as they made the sound of a flowing river. When the wind stopped, I could see the shapes and designs of the leaves on the stems with the deep blue sky as a dramatic backdrop. They were symmetrically balanced rows of leaves. I immediately pulled out my notebook and sketched the designs. The baroque freshwater pearls used in this design represent the leaves as they sprout on a twig, while their shape and pearly luster make a lovely and soothing shape that can easily be made as a pendant for a necklace.

INSTRUCTIONS

1. Cut the 24-gauge wire into two pieces that are each 12" (30.5cm) in length.

2. Insert a 9x5mm baroque shaped freshwater pearl and slide it onto the center of one of the 12" (30.5cm) of wire. Hold the pearl with your fingers and with your other hand cross the wires to form an X leaving about 2mm of space between the pearl and the X. Use the tip of the flat-nose pliers to hold the wire above the X and twist it twice.

3. Insert a pearl onto each of the two wires so they are next to each other and cross the wires to form an X. Hold the two pearls between your fingers, and use the tip of the flat-nose pliers to twist the wire above the X twice.

4. Repeat step 3 twice, and then make a wrapped loop (page 152) with one of the wires, wrapping it around the stem three times, but do not cut the remaining wire.

5. Use one of the two wires and wrap it over the two closest pearls then around the stem three times, wrap over the next two pearls and around the stem three times, wrap over the third pair of pearls then around the stem three times, and then cut off the remaining wire and make it snug around the stem.

6. Repeat step 5 with the second wire, wrapping the wire in the opposite direction so it forms an X shape in between each pair of pearls, but only wrap it twice around the stem instead of three times.

7. Open the loop on an earwire and attach the wrapped loop, and then close the earwire.

LEVEL
Intermediate

LENGTH
1¾" (4.4cm)

TOOLS
Ruler
Wire cutters
Chain-nose pliers
Flat-nose pliers
Round-nose pliers

MATERIALS
24" (61cm) of 24-gauge sterling silver wire (soft)
Fourteen 9x5mm (sizes vary) baroque shaped top-drilled fresh-water pearls
Two sterling silver earwires

SEPTEMBER LEAVES NECKLACE

September is a month of transitions. It is the time when late summer becomes early autumn, the days become shorter, and the weather is not sure whether it wants to be hot or cool. Students return to school, summer casual becomes casual professional, and green leaves begin to show spots of yellow. This necklace uses Fukinsei, a Japanese design principle of asymmetric balance that is often described as "unbalanced harmony." It has two strands of different lengths; one has one segment of gems and the other has two, and neither is positioned right at the center. Yet it maintains a remarkable poise and natural balance. The green tourmaline gems include subtle shades of yellow to represent the changing colors of the leaves in September.

LEVEL
Intermediate

LENGTH
17½" (44.5cm) inner strand; 18½" (47cm)
   outer strand

TOOLS
Ruler
Wire cutters
Chain-nose pliers
Round-nose pliers
Materials:
27¾" (70.6cm) of 4x3mm sterling silver
   cable chain
18" (45.8cm) of 24 gauge sterling silver
   wire (soft)
Twelve 9x4mm faceted, center-drilled,
   marquise-shaped green tourmaline gems
Sterling silver toggle bar and clasp
Two 4mm sterling silver jump rings

INSTRUCTIONS

1. Cut the 27¾" (70.6cm) of 4x3mm cable chain into 5 separate pieces in the following lengths: 3" (7.7cm); 4½" (11.5cm); 4¾" (12.1cm); 5½" (14cm); and 9" (23cm).

2. Cut the 18" (45.8cm) of 24 gauge wire into 12 pieces that are each 1½" (3.8cm) in length.

3. Use a 1½" (3.8cm) length of wire and a 9x4mm green tourmaline gem, and make a wrapped loop gem link (page 153) with one open loop and one closed loop.

4. Make a second wrapped loop gem link with a tourmaline gem, with an open and closed loop, and attach the open loop to the closed link of the first wrapped loop link.

5. Repeat step 4 twice. Leave the end of the fourth wrapped loop open so the four wrapped loop links are attached with open loops on the outer ends as shown in figure 1.

6. Repeat steps 3 to 5 twice, so you end up with three of the segments that are each composed of 4 linked gems and shown in figure 1.

7. To make the longer strand of this two-strand necklace, attach the last link of the 4½"(11.5cm) length of chain to the open loop end of one of the gem segments. Attach the opposite open loop of the gem segment to a 3" (7.7cm) length of chain. Then, attach the opposite end link of the 3" (7.7cm) length of chain to an open loop end of another gem segment, and attach the opposite open loop of the gem segment to the 5½" (14cm) length of chain. See figure 1.

8. For the shorter strand of the necklace, attach an last link of the 9" (23cm) length of chain to the open loop end of the final gem segment, and attach the opposite open loop of the gem segment to the last link of the 4¾" (12.1cm) length of chain.

9. Open a 4mm jump ring and attach the last link of the strand with a 4½" (11.5cm) length of chain and the last link of the 9" (23cm) length of chain, and the loop of the clasp, and then close the jump ring.

10. Open another jump ring, and attach the opposite end links of the two strands of chain and the loop of the toggle bar, then close the jump ring.

FIGURE 1

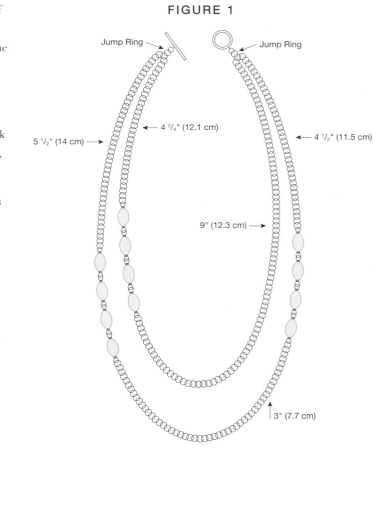

Jump Ring

Jump Ring

← 4 ¾" (12.1 cm)

5 ½" (14 cm) →

← 4 ½" (11.5 cm)

9" (12.3 cm) →

3" (7.7 cm)

SPROUTING SPRIG NECKLACE

Nature's designs are often balanced, but not perfectly, rigidly symmetric like manmade designs. Nature is not perfect, and it likes to have fun with color and shapes. The Sprouting Sprig Necklace reproduces this "perfect imperfection." Just as every leaf on a stem is not always the same color as the next, the golden citrine and green peridot of this design echo the variation of color that occurs in nature.

LEVEL
Advanced

LENGTH
29¾" (75.6cm); Pendant: 1¾"x1½"
(4.5cmx3.2cm)

TOOLS
Ruler

Wire cutters

Chain-nose pliers

Flat-nose pliers

Round-nose pliers

Goggles

MATERIALS
25" (63.6cm) of 24-gauge 14k gold-filled
wire (soft). As always, if you prefer a
different length, adjust the the necklace
chain accordingly.

Seven 12x8mm (approximate size) faceted,
top-drilled teardrop citrine gems

One 8x5mm faceted, top-drilled, teardrop
peridot gem

29" (73.8cm) of 1.6mm 14k gold-filled, flat
cable chain

One 14k gold-filled filigree clasp

Two 4mm 14k gold-filled jump rings

INSTRUCTIONS

1. Insert one of the 12x8mm citrine gems onto the 25" (63.6cm) of 24-gauge wire and slide it to the center of the wire.

2. Hold the gem with your fingers, and with your other hand, cross the wires over each other at the point of the gem to form an X, leaving about 2mm of space between the gem and the X. Then, hold the wire at the X with the tip of the flat-nose pliers and twist it three times.

3. String a citrine gem onto each of the two wires. Then hold the center gem and the gem on the left side and pull the wire from the left gem over to the right side. Then, hold the center gem and the gem on the right side and pull the wire from the right gem over to the left side so the wire forms an X with about 2mm between the gems and the X. Hold the gems between your fingers, then hold the wire at the X with the flat-nose pliers and twist it five times. Don't worry if the gems are little loose on the wires, you will wrap them with wire later.

4. Insert a citrine gem onto one of the wires and hold the gem at ¼" (6mm) away from the stem and tilt the gem so the wire bends to a right angle and the sharp tip of the gem points toward the stem. Pull the wire towards the center of the stem so it makes the shape of a small triangle as shown in figure 1.

5. Hold the three gems between your thumb and index finger, and with the thumb and index finger from your other hand, hold the one gem on the triangle-shaped wire. Pinch the tip of the triangle shape closest to the stem. and twist the wire gently three times. The reason you do not just hold and twist the gem is that the force of the wire twisting at the weakest part of the gem could cause it to break.

6. Repeat steps 4 and 5 on the right side, and then use the flat-nose pliers to twist the two wires four times to form the center stem.

7. Repeat steps 4 and 5 on the left side, and then twist the wires twice to form the center stem. Then, repeat steps 4 and 5 on the right side again.

8. Twist the wires twice, then insert the teardrop peridot gem onto the wire on the left side. That wire will serve as the stem. Then, wrap the other wire over the peridot gem and around the stem wire three times.

9. Bend one wire to a right angle perpendicular to the pendant and towards the back, and use the wide part of the jaws of the round-nose pliers to make a basic wrapped loop, wrapping twice around the stem. Do not cut off the end. (Ignore the other wire as you do this.)

10. Use the remainder of this wire to wrap around the stem and branches. Wrap your way down, focusing this wire on the stems and branches on one side of the pendant. When you run out of wire, be sure to use the chain-nose pliers to make the end of the wire snug against the stem.

11. Use the other wire to wrap around the stems and branches, focusing on the opposite side of the pendant.

12. Thread the 29" (73.8cm) of cable chain into the loop of the branch.

13. Open a jump ring and attach the last link of one side of the chain and the loop of the filigree clasp. Close the jump ring.

14. Open the other jump ring, and attach the last link of the opposite side of the chain to the filigree clasp. Close the jump ring.

FIGURE 1
(numbers indicate twists)

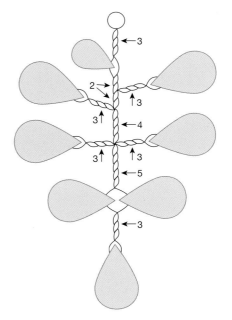

Wisterias are some of my favorite flowers. They are popular in Japan, where they grow on vines up to twenty-five feet high. They grow on fences and are especially lovely when they grow over arches that people construct just for them. They have pleasantly fragrant bunches of cascading flower clusters in soft shades of white, pink, lilac blue, bluish purple, or purple. Inspired by wisterias, these earrings use rose quartz and pink amethyst gems to perfectly reproduce the delicate colors of the flowers.

LEVEL
Intermediate

LENGTH
1½" (3.8cm)

TOOLS
Ruler
Wire cutters
Chain-nose pliers
Round-nose pliers

MATERIALS
2½" (6.4cm) of 4x3mm 14k gold-filled cable chain (two 8-link lengths)
Two 14k gold-filled earwires
75½" (192.8cm) of 26 gauge 14k gold-filled wire (soft)
Eight 10x8mm faceted, flat, oval rose quartz gems
Eight 4mm faceted rondelle pink amethyst gems
Thirty-eight 3mm faceted rondelle rose quartz gems

INSTRUCTIONS

1. Cut the 4x3mm cable chain to two 8-link lengths (1³⁄₁₆" [3cm] each), and attach an end link of each to an earwire. Close the earwire loop.

2. Cut the 75½" (190.5cm) of 26 gauge wire to 38 lengths that are each 1¼" (3.2cm), 8 lengths that are each 1½" (3.8cm), and 8 lengths that are each 2" (5.1cm), and then make them all into a headpins.

3. Insert the thirty-eight 3mm rondelle rose quartz gems onto the 1¼" (3.2cm) length headpins, the eight 4mm rondelle pink amethyst gems onto the 1½" (3.8cm) length headpins, and the eight 10x8mm oval rose quartz gems onto the 2" (5.1cm) headpins, and make all of them into open loops (page 152).

4. Beginning on the bottom chain link of one of the earrings, attach the gems to the chain as shown in figure 1. First attach one 3mm faceted rondelle rose quartz gem to the bottom chain link, then two rondelle rose quartz gems to the second link, with one on each side of the link.

5. Attach four rose quartz rondelle gems to the 3rd link, with two on each side of the link, and then four rose quartz rondelle gems to the 4th link also, with two on each side of the link.

6. Attach two 4mm rondelle pink amethyst gems to the top of the same fourth link with one on each side of the link, then attach two more 4mm pink amethyst gems to the 5th link with one on each side.

7. Attach two rose quartz rondelle gems to the 6th link, with one on each side.

8. Attach two of the 10x8mm flat, oval rose quartz gems to the 7th link, with one on each side, and then attach two more 10x8mm rose quartz gems to the 8th (top) link, with one on each side of the link.

9. Attach 4 rose quartz rondelle gems on the 8th (top) link above the oval rose quartz gems, with two on each side of the link, and then attach two rose quartz rondelle gems to the earwire loop with one on each side.

10. Repeat steps 4 through 9 for the second earring.

FIGURE 1

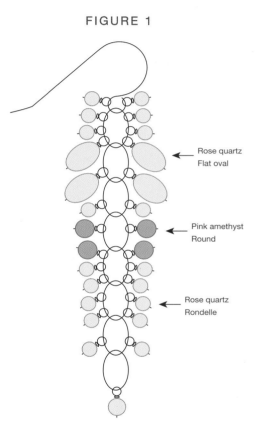

Rose quartz
Flat oval

Pink amethyst
Round

Rose quartz
Rondelle

CHAPTER SEVEN

CREATURES OF THE EARTH JEWELRY DESIGNS

With advances in the technology of deep-sea exploration, scientists are discovering many new forms of life we have never seen before. Photos of amazing creatures in shapes and forms that we never knew existed are available in books and on websites. A photo of a cute, transparent baby octopus with tiny tentacles inspired this necklace pendant. The large yellow citrine stone is a happy and cheerful light color and is translucent like the baby octopus. This is a fun design that I like to wear with casual outfits, but it also works with professional outfits or over a sweater.

LEVEL
Easy

LENGTH
18¾" (47.7cm)

TOOLS
Ruler

Wire cutters

Chain-nose pliers

Round-nose pliers

MATERIALS
15" (38.2cm) of 26-gauge 14k gold-filled
 wire (soft)

Six 3mm faceted rondelle aquamarine gems

Six 3mm faceted rondelle peridot gems

4" (10.2cm) of 20-gauge 14k gold-filled wire
 (soft)

One 22x28mm (approximate) citrine
 nugget gem

Two 12-link lengths of 20x14mm 14k gold-
 filled hammered cable chain

Two 7mm 14k gold-filled jump rings

14k gold-filled toggle and bar clasp

INSTRUCTIONS

1. Cut the 15" (38.2cm) of 26-gauge wire into 12 pieces that are each 1¼" (3.2cm) in length, and make them all into headpins.

2. Insert a rondelle gem onto each of the headpins and then make a wrapped loop (page 152) on each.

3. Bend the 4" (10.2cm) of 20 gauge wire at 1⅜" (3.5cm) and use the wider part of the jaw of the round-nose pliers to make an open loop (page 152) that is about 4mm in diameter, and then insert the 12 rondelle aquamarine and peridot gems alternating them (aquamarine, peridot, aquamarine, peridot, etc.) and then close it with a wrapped loop.

4. Insert the 22x28mm citrine nugget gem onto the stem above the wrapped loop with the rondelle gems, and make another open loop and attach it to the end links of the two 20x14mm hammered cable chains and close the wrapped loop.

5. Open a 7mm jump ring and insert the last link of the 20x14mm cable chain and the loop of the bar clasp, then close the jump ring.

6. Open the other jump ring and insert the last link on the opposite end of the 20x14mm cable chain and the loop on the toggle, and then close the jump ring.

BIRD MOTIF EARRINGS

This earring design was inspired by the ornamental motifs of ancient cultures. Natural forms were represented in rigid geometric and symmetric designs. Modeled after the shape of a bird, this design uses mirror symmetry, which happens when the left side of the object is exactly like the right side. The dangling gemstones add movement, and the distinctive golden chain links in the crinkle design add sparkle that reflects off the marquise-shaped green tourmaline gems.

INSTRUCTIONS

1. Cut the 24-gauge wire to six pieces that are 2" (5.1cm) in length and one that is 2¾" (7cm) in length.

2. Make each of the six 2" (5.1cm) lengths into a headpin, and insert each of them into a green tourmaline gem. Make an open loop (page 152) on each.

3. Cut the crinkle chain in the following lengths: four one-link lengths; four three-link lengths; four five-link lengths.

4. Use one of the 2¾" (7cm) lengths of wire and with your round-nose pliers bend it at ¾" (1.9cm) and make an open loop, then insert the end links of the crinkle chains onto the loop in the following order: 3-link, 1-link, 5-link. Then, close the loop.

5. Insert a gem onto the stem, make an open loop, then slide the crinkle chain into the loop as above (3-link, 1-link, 5-link), and then close the loop.

6. Open a 4mm jump ring, insert the end links of the 3-link chains, and insert the loop of an earwire, and then close the jump ring.

7. Insert the end links of the 5-link chains onto one of the open loops of the gems you made in step 2, and then close the wrapped loop.

8. Use another gem with an open loop and attach it to one of the dangling 1-link crinkle chains, and do the same on the opposite end.

9. Repeat steps 4 through 8 for the second earring.

LEVEL
Intermediate

LENGTH
2⅜" (6cm)

TOOLS
Ruler

Chain-nose pliers

Round-nose pliers

MATERIALS
Eight 9x5mm center-drilled, marquise-
  shaped green tourmaline gems

Two 14k gold-filled earwires

8½" (21.7cm) of 5x2mm gold-filled crinkle
  chain

13½" (34.3cm) of 24-gauge gold-filled wire
  (soft)

Two 4mm 14k gold-filled jump rings

JELLYFISH EARRINGS

I have to admit that I love jellyfish. I first became captivated by them on a visit to an aquarium. I found it so relaxing to watch them floating and moving so gently and gracefully in the water. Some look like transparent flowers detached from the earth, drifting and pulsating in the currents. I saw tiny jellyfish that had quicker movements, yet still they moved in such an ethereal and tranquil way. Inspired by these tiny jellyfish, these earrings use large round citrine stones to represent their translucent bodies, while the lightly colored aquamarine, pink amethyst, and rose quartz gems represent their tiny tentacles.

LEVEL
Easy

LENGTH
1⅜" (3.5cm)

TOOLS
Ruler

Wire cutters

Chain-nose pliers

Round-nose pliers

MATERIALS
Two 14k gold-filled earwires

Twenty-six 1½" (3.8cm) 14k gold-filled ball
   headpins

4½" (11.5cm) of 24 gauge gold-filled wire (soft)

Two 14mm round faceted citrine gems

Eight 3mm faceted rondelle aquamarine gems

Eight 3mm faceted rondelle citrine gems

Eight 4mm faceted rondelle rose quartz gems

Two 3mm faceted rondelle pink amethyst gems

INSTRUCTIONS

1. Insert a rondelle gem onto each of the twenty-six 1½" (3.8cm) headpins and make a wrapped loop on each of them.

2. Cut the 4½"(11.5cm) 24-gauge wire in half into two lengths that are each 2¼" (5.7cm).

3. Bend the 2¼" (5.7cm) wire at ⅝" (1.6cm) and use the wider part of the jaw of the round-nose pliers to make an open loop (page 152) that is about 4mm in diameter, and then insert 13 of the rondelle gems in the following order: aquamarine, rose quartz, citrine, aquamarine, rose quartz, citrine, pink amethyst, citrine, rose quartz, aquamarine, citrine, rose quartz, aquamarine. Then, close the wrapped loop.

4. Insert the 14mm round citrine gem onto the stem above the wrapped loop with the gems, and make another wrapped loop.

5. Open the loop on the earwire, insert the top loop, and then close the loop.

6. Repeat steps 3 through 5 for the second earring.

PEACOCK FEATHER EARRINGS

Peacock feathers are amazing natural works of art. In this earring design, chains cut to different lengths recreate the beautiful pattern on the feather of the peacock. The peacock is associated with pride because of the way the male bird displays its beautiful and colorful feathers to attract the female bird. Similarly, the rutilated quartz proudly displays its unique and golden inclusions.

INSTRUCTIONS

1. Cut the 20½" (52cm) of 1.6mm cable chain as follows:

   1cm—Four lengths, 1.4cm—Four lengths, 1.7cm—Four lengths
   2cm—Four lengths, 2.3cm—Four lengths, 2.5cm—Two lengths

2. Cut the 11" (28cm) 20-gauge wire in half into two 5½" (14cm) lengths and then make a curved shape on the each by gently wrapping the center of each wire around a mandrel or any round item that is about 3" in circumference (1" in diameter) so it makes a U shape.

3. Use a U-shaped wire and cross the ends of the wire so they make an X with one wire extending 1½" (3.8cm) past the X and the other ¼" (7mm). Use flat-nose pliers to hold the wire above the X and twist it twice, and then make a wrapped loop (page 152). Be aware that this will require a little more strength than usual since this is hard wire. Hard wire is used in this design so that the earring will keep its curved shape.

4. Use the 4mm jump rings to attach the lengths of chain onto the curved wire in the following order: 1cm, 1.4cm, 1.7cm, 2cm, 2.3cm, 2.5cm, 2.3cm, 2cm, 1.7cm, 1.4cm, 1cm.

5. Open the earwire loop and attach the loop of the 20-gauge wire teardrop, then attach the two links of the 4x3mm cable chain, and then close the earwire loop.

6. Insert a 1½" (3.8cm) headpin into a rutilated quartz gem, make an open loop (page 152), attach it to the end of the 2-link cable chain, and then close the wrapped loop.

7. Repeat steps 3 through 6 for the second earring.

LEVEL
Intermediate

LENGTH
3³⁄₁₆" (8.1cm)

TOOLS
Ruler

Wire cutters

Chain-nose pliers

Flat-nose pliers

Round-nose pliers

Mandrel (optional) or round item that is about 3" in circumference (1" in diameter)

MATERIALS
20½" (52.1cm) of 1.6mm 14k gold-filled cable chain

11" (28cm) of 20-gauge 14k gold-filled wire (hard)

Twenty-two 4mm 14k gold-filled jump rings

Two 14k gold-filled earwires

Two 1½" (3.8cm) 14k gold-filled ball headpins

Two 14x10mm faceted, flat oval, center-drilled rutilated quartz gems

¾" (1.9cm) of 4x3mm 14k gold-filled flat cable chain (two 2-link lengths)

BUTTERFLY NECKLACE

The unusual life cycle of butterflies symbolizes birth and renewal—they change from eggs, to caterpillars, to a pupal stage where they actually liquefy and experience a metamorphosis, to finally reemerge as winged creatures. A butterfly is a perfect example of the mirror symmetry found in nature's creatures. Here I've used two separate links of large chain to represent their grand upper wings and amethyst gems to represent their ethereal lower wings.

LEVEL
Intermediate

LENGTH
17½" (44.5cm)

TOOLS
Ruler

Wire cutter

Chain-nose pliers

Round-nose pliers

MATERIALS
10½" (26.7cm) of 24-gauge sterling silver wire (soft)

Six 4mm sterling silver jump rings

2 separate closed links of 20x14mm ribbed sterling silver cable chain

Four 3mm faceted rondelle amethyst gems

Two 7x7mm faceted center-drilled teardrop amethyst gems

14⁹⁄₁₆" (37.1cm) of 1.6mm sterling silver flat cable chain

One sterling silver filigree clasp

INSTRUCTIONS

1. Cut the 10½" (26.7cm) of 24 gauge wire to three lengths that are 1¼" (3.2cm) each, and two lengths that are 1½" (3.8cm) each, and you will be left with one 2" (5.1cm) length of wire. Make the three 1¼" (3.2cm) lengths and the two 1½" (3.8cm) length wires into headpins.

2. Open a 4mm jump ring and insert a 20x14mm cable chain link, then close the jump ring.

3. Open another jump ring and attach it to the second 20x14mm cable chain link then close the jump ring.

4. Use the 2" (5.1cm) length of the 24-gauge wire with a 3mm rondelle amethyst gem to make a wrapped loop gem link (page 153) with an open loop on one side and a wrapped loop on the opposite side. Insert the open loop into the two jump rings that are attached to the two 20x14mm cable chain links and close it with a wrapped loop.

5. Insert the three 1¼" (3.2cm) headpins into the 3mm amethyst gems and make each into an open loop, and then attach each of them onto the bottom loop of the wrapped loop gem link and close each with a wrapped loop.

6. Cut the 1.6mm cable chain to two lengths that are each 7¼" (18.5cm). Open a jump ring and insert the end link of the 7¼" (18.5cm) 1.6mm cable chain and one of the 20x14mm cable chain links, and then close the jump ring. Open another jump ring and attach the other 7¼" (18.5cm) length chain on the opposite 20x14mm cable chain link, and close the jump ring.

7. Insert the two 1½" (3.8cm) headpins into the 7x7mm teardrop amethyst gems and make an open loop on each.

8. Attach one of the 7x7mm amethyst gems onto one of the 20x14mm cable chain links and then close it with a wrapped loop. Attach the remaining 7x7mm amethyst gem to the other 20x14mm cable link.

9. Open a jump ring and attach the end link of the 1.6mm chain and a loop of the filigree clasp, then close the jump ring. Open the last jump ring and attach the last link of the opposite end of the necklace and the loop on the opposite end of the filigree clasp, then close the jump ring.

BEE NECKLACE

I always enjoy watching bees go from flower to flower, dipping in for sweet, fragrant nectar. They hover over the flowers and bump against them just enough to pollinate them. Some bees become covered in pollen as they visit a flower. I've used wire to make the shape of a bee with wings in motion as it hovers over a violet flower made of the three rondelle iolite gems.

INSTRUCTIONS

Note: If you have experience working with hard wire, I recommend using it for this project because it will hold the shape of the bee better. However, if you are not experienced with the hard wire, I recommend that you practice first with a soft or inexpensive wire before you use the sterling silver hard wire. If you make a mistake with soft wire, you can easily straighten it out and then bend it back to the shape you want, but once you bend hard wire, it can break if you try to straighten or bend it again.

I've used #400 grit wet/dry sandpaper to sand the bee shape and give the silver a textured look, and to provide you with an introduction to the world of metalsmithing. The sandpaper can only be used on precious metals, such as sterling silver, gold or platinum. It should not be used on gold-filled or gold plated because it can remove the gold around the core metal. The textured look will also remove any scratches and give the piece dimension.

1. Use the chain-nose pliers to bend the 10" (25.5cm) 20-gauge wire at 4½" (11.5cm) into a V shape, then use the flat-nose pliers to gently squeeze the bend so the wire is creased and parallel. Don't squeeze too hard, as this could scratch the wire or make it weak at the bend.

2. Slightly separate the wires with your fingers, hold the wire at ¾" (1.9cm) from the crease and slide the jaws of the chain-nose pliers in between, and gently pull the wire open on each side
so the tip of the wire makes a leaf shape and the wires cross in an X.

3. Hold the leaf shape with the chain-nose pliers perpendicular to the leaf, and use the flat-nose pliers to twist the wire at the X twice (at about ¾" [1.9cm]).

LEVEL
Advanced

LENGTH
16" (40.7cm) to 18" (45.8cm);
(This necklace is adjustable.)
Pendant: 1⅜"x1" (3.5x2.5cm)

TOOLS
Ruler

Wire cutters

Flat-nose pliers

Chain-nose pliers

Round-nose pliers

Goggles (you will work with long pieces of wire)

#400 grit—wet/dry sandpaper (optional) to
   provide a matte finish

MATERIALS
10" (25.5cm) of 20-gauge sterling silver wire
   (hard or soft, see Note)

20" (50.8cm) of 26-gauge sterling silver wire

15½" (39.4cm) of 1.6mm sterling silver flat cable chain

2" (5.1cm) of 4x3mm sterling silver flat cable chain

One sterling silver spring-ring clasp

Four 1½" (3.8cm) sterling silver ball headpins

Two 4mm sterling silver jump rings

Four 3mm faceted rondelle iolite gems

4. Hold the leaf shape, which will become the abdomen of the bee, between your fingers with the tip pointing toward you and bend the longer wire down so it makes a 45-degree angle to the abdomen. Then, use the tip of the chain-nose pliers to bend the wire to a V shape at ¾" (1.9cm), and then use the flat-nose pliers to gently squeeze the bend so the wire is creased, as in step 1.

5. Slightly separate the wires with your fingers and hold the wire and slide the jaws of the chain-nose pliers in between. Gently pull the wire open on each side to shape the wire into the wing just as you shaped the abdomen.

6. Hold the stem, which is becoming the body of the bee (technically called a thorax), and use your fingers from your other hand to bend the new leaf shape (which will become a wing) and the abdomen close together. Then hold the wing and the abdomen between your fingers and use the flat-nose pliers to twist the wire at the X twice. This wing should be the same size as the abdomen.

7. Hold the wing with the tip pointing toward you and bend the same wire down and at ¹¹/₁₆" (1.7cm), bend the wire with the tip of the chain-nose pliers. Then, use the flat-nose pliers to crease the wire. This wing and the remaining 2 wings will be made gradually smaller. Repeat steps 5 and 6 to shape this wing.

8. Repeat step 7 to make the third wing, but this time make the bend at ⅝" (1.6cm).

9. Repeat step 7 to make the fourth and final wing and this time make the bend at ⅜" (1cm). After you complete this wing and twist the wire twice, cut the shorter wire close to the stem and make it snug.

10. Use the remaining wire to make a wrapped loop (page 152), which will become the head, wrap the wire around the stem twice, cut off any remaining wire, and then use the tip of the chain-nose pliers to make it snug.

11. Use your fingers to adjust the wings and body to make the shape of the bee, and then use the chain-nose or flat-nose pliers to slightly twist the top wing so it is perpendicular to the other wings. This wing will be the bail that holds the necklace chain. Insert the tip of the round-nose pliers into the cusp of the top wing and gently press to round it out so that it hangs smoothly on the chain and doesn't get stuck on it. Don't squeeze too tight, as this could break the wire.

12. If you want to add texture and remove any scratches, use the sandpaper to sand the wings, body and head of the bee. (This step is optional.)

13. Use the 20" (50.8cm) of 26-gauge wire and bend the shape of a V at ½" (1.3cm) and hook the V into the abdomen of the bee (I know this sounds painful). Use the chain-nose pliers to wrap the short tail around the stem and then make it snug.

14. Use the long wire to wrap around the stem to form the shape of the bee's body. Once you begin wrapping the wire around the body you shouldn't stop until you're done, because the wire should be tight; if you stop before it is secured, it could unwind and lose its shape.

15. Begin by wrapping around the stem in a coiling fashion between the abdomen and the first wing five times, wrap once inside the first wing, wrap around the stem between the first and second wing 7 times, wrap once inside the second wing, and then wrap between the third and fourth wing three times. Don't wrap between the wing and the head yet. Use the wire to work your way back down, wrapping around the body of the bee and filling in where you think it needs more body shape, and then work your way back up to the top.

16. Wrap the wire around the stem between the top wing and the head three times, wrap a loose loop around one side of the top wing, insert the wire in the loop like you as if tying a knot, wrap the wire once around the stem and cut off any

remaining wire, and use the tip of the chain-nose pliers to make it snug. The knot will hold it securely so it doesn't come unwound.

17. Insert an iolite gem onto each of the four 1½" (3.8cm) headpins and make an open loop on each.

18. Attach three of the gems onto the head of the bee and close them each with a wrapped loop. These represent the flower.

19. Open a 4mm jump ring and insert the last link of the 15½" (39.4cm) 1.6mm flat cable chain and the loop of the spring ring clasp and close the jump ring. Insert the chain into the top wing of the bee.

20. Open another jump ring and insert last link on the opposite end of the 1.6mm chain and the last link of the 2" (5.1cm) 4x3mm cable chain, and then close the jump ring.

21. Attach the last iolite gem on a headpin to the end of the 2" (5.1cm) 4x3mm chain and close the wrapped loop.

Fireflies, also known as lightning bugs, are another one of nature's collection of fascinating and enchanting creatures. They actually produce light! It is especially exciting to see bunches of them flashing and glowing in the night like twinkling little stars. I've used sterling silver, the most reflective of all metals, and rainbow moonstone to represent the flickering light these glowing insects produce. This pendant design can be adapted easily to make matching earrings by hanging the piece on earwires.

LEVEL
Easy

LENGTH
16" (40.7cm) to 18" (45.8cm) Adjustable

TOOLS
Ruler

Wire Cutters

Chain-nose pliers

Round-nose pliers

MATERIALS
Ten 1½" (3.8cm) sterling silver ball
   headpins

Eight 3mm faceted rondelle rainbow
   moonstone gems

One link of 20x14mm ribbed sterling silver
   cable chain

One 9x7mm center-drilled faceted oval
   rainbow moonstone gem

15½" (39.4cm) of 1.6mm sterling silver flat
   cable chain

2" (5.1cm) of 4x3mm sterling silver flat
   cable chain

One sterling silver spring ring clasp

Three 4mm sterling silver jump rings

INSTRUCTIONS

1. Insert one of the 1½" (3.8cm) headpins into a 3mm rondelle rainbow moonstone gem, make an open loop, attach it onto the one link of 20x14mm cable chain, close the loop, then do the same with 7 more headpins and 7 rondelle rainbow moonstone gems.

2. Insert a headpin into the center-drilled oval rainbow moonstone gem and make an open loop. Attach the loop onto the 20x14mm ribbed cable chain in between the 8 rondelle gems (4 on each side of it), and close the loop.

3. Open a 4mm jump ring, attach the top of the 20x14mm cable chain link and then close it.

4. Thread the 1.6mm cable chain through the jump ring.

5. Open another 4mm jump ring, attach it to the last link of the 1.6mm cable chain, insert the loop of the spring ring clasp, and then close the jump ring.

6. Open the last jump ring, attach it to the last link on the opposite end of the 1.6mm flat cable chain, insert the 2" (5.1cm) 4x3mm cable chain, and then close the jump ring.

7. Use the remaining headpin and the rondelle rainbow moonstone gem to make an open loop and attach it on the last link of the 4x3mm cable chain.

CHAPTER EIGHT

NATURE'S BOUNTY JEWELRY DESIGNS

CLUSTER BERRIES EARRINGS

Many berries have colors that strongly resemble gemstones. I enjoy visiting farmer's markets and take particular pleasure in the resplendent and bright colors of radiant red raspberries, shimmering blueberries, and glistening blackberries. Berries reflect the afternoon sunlight and sparkle with the misty drops of dew. These black spinel earrings bear a striking resemblance to blackberries. You can use sparkling rondelle gems in many other refreshing colors to make this sumptuous and lively design.

LEVEL
Easy

LENGTH
1½" (3.8cm)

TOOLS
Ruler
Wire cutters
Chain-nose pliers
Round-nose pliers

MATERIALS
3" (7.6cm) of 4x3mm 14k gold-filled flat cable chain (two 10-link lengths)
50" (127cm) of 26-gauge 14k gold-filled wire (soft)
4" (10.2cm) of 24-gauge 14k gold-filled wire (soft)
42 3mm faceted rondelle black spinel garnet gems
Two 14k gold-filled earwires

INSTRUCTIONS

1. Cut the 3" (7.6cm) of 4x3mm cable chain into two pieces that each have 10 links (1⅜" [3.5cm] each).

2. Cut the 24-gauge wire in half to two lengths at 2" (5.1cm) each, and put them aside.

3. Cut the 26-gauge wire into 40 pieces that are each 1¼" (3.2cm), and make all of them into headpins.

4. Insert the gems onto the headpins and then make an open loop (page 152) on each of them.

5. Attach two of the gems with open loops to each of the 10 links of chain, attaching one on each side of the link.

6. Use one of the 2" (5.1cm) 24-gauge wires and a gem to make wrapped loop gem links (page 152) with one open loop and one closed wrapped loop.

7. Attach the two last links of the chain with the gems onto the open loop of the wrapped loop gem link and close it with a wrapped loop.

8. Open an earwire loop and insert the opposite end of the wrapped loop gem link, and then close the earwire.

9. Repeat steps 5 to 8 for the second earring.

GRAPEVINE NECKLACE

In New York City, any bit of outdoor space is extremely coveted and very valuable. Last summer, I sublet my apartment so I could stay in another sublet apartment with a tiny backyard garden. The back of the building was covered with green leaves, which to my pleasant surprise were actually part of a vibrant and healthy grapevine. Here, I've re-created the gorgeous bunches of grapes on that vine in aquamarine.

INSTRUCTIONS

1. Cut the 20-gauge wire into 7 pieces that are each 2" (5.1cm) in length and 4 pieces that are each 1¾" (4.5cm) in length and make them all into headpins.

2. Insert the 7" (5.1cm) headpins onto the seven 20x16mm aqua-marine nuggets, and then make an open loop (page 152) on each.

3. Attach one of the aquamarine gems with an open loop to the end link of the 1¾" (4.5cm) of 4x3.5mm cable chain (14-links) and close it with a Wrapped Loop (page 152).

4. Attach another aquamarine gem to the sixth link of the same small chain, counting from the link where the first gemstone is attached.

5. Attach a second aquamarine gem to the same sixth link on the chain, but on the opposite side of the link.

6. Attach two aquamarine gems to the ninth link on the chain, with one on each side of the link, as on the sixth link.

7. Repeat step 6 on the twelfth link of the chain.

8. Insert the four 1¾" (4.4cm) headpins onto the four 14x12mm aquamarine gems and make a wrapped loop on each.

9. Open the 8mm jump ring and insert two of the four 14x12mm gems, then insert the end of the 4x3.5mm (14-link) chain that does not have a gem, then insert the remaining two 14x12mm aquamarine gems and finally, insert both ends of the large 20x14mm ribbed cable chain and then close the jump ring.

   Note: This is a closed chain necklace with no clasp, which means you put it on over your head. If you prefer to have a longer chain, you can extend the size of the 20x14mm ribbed cable chain.

LEVEL
Intermediate

LENGTH
28" (71.2cm); pendant: 2¾"x1⅜" (7x3.5cm)

TOOLS
Wire cutters

Chain-nose pliers

Round-nose pliers

Ruler

MATERIALS
21" (53.5cm) of 20-gauge sterling silver wire (soft)

Seven 20x16mm faceted aquamarine nuggets (approximate size)

28" (71cm) of 20x14mm sterling silver ribbed cable chain

1¾" (4.5cm) of 4x3.5mm sterling silver cable chain (14-links)

Four 14x12mm faceted aquamarine nuggets (approximate size)

One 8mm sterling silver jump ring

CURRANT NECKLACE

Currants are sweet summer berries that look like tiny ruby-red grapes. The ruby gemstones are an excellent gem that replicates the color of fresh currants. This elegant design, in which you are literally "wrapped in gems," is gracefully balanced, dainty, and delicate, while the red ruby gems add a bit of bold color. This is a great necklace for business meetings or a fancy dinner and a night out on the town. You can easily substitute the rubies with any gem.

LEVEL
Easy

LENGTH
16" (40.7cm) to 18" (45.8cm) adjustable

TOOLS
Ruler

Wire cutters

Chain-nose pliers

Round-nose pliers

MATERIALS
Two 4mm 14k gold-filled jump rings

One 14k gold-filled spring ring clasp

15½" (39.4 cm) of 1.6mm 14k gold-filled
   flat cable chain

2" (5.1cm) of 4x3mm 14k gold-filled flat
   cable chain

43" (110cm) of 26-gauge gold-filled wire
   (soft)

Thirty-three 3mm faceted rondelle ruby
   gems

One 13x10mm faceted, top-drilled
   teardrop ruby gem

INSTRUCTIONS

1. Open a 4mm jump ring and attach the loop of the spring ring clasp and an end link of the 15½" (39.4 cm) of 1.6mm cable chain, then close the jump ring.

2. Open another 4mm jump ring and attach the opposite end of the 15½" (39.4 cm) of 1.6mm chain and an end link of the 2" (5.1cm) of 4x3mm cable chain, then close the jump ring.

3. Cut a 1¾" (4.4cm) length from the 26-gauge wire, insert it into the 13x10mm ruby gem and make a top-drilled open gem loop.

4. Fold the 15½" (39.4 cm) of 1.6mm chain in half (not including the attached chain or clasp) and attach the open loop of the 13x10mm ruby to the center link of the chain, and then close the loop.

5. Cut the remaining 26-gauge wire into 33 pieces that are each 1¼" (3.2cm) in length, and make all of them into headpins. Then, attach the rondelle ruby gems and make an open loop on each of them.

6. Starting from the centerpiece gem, attach the open loops of the rondelle ruby gems onto the 15½" (39.4 cm) of 1.6mm chain at every half inch. There should be seven links between each gem. Be sure to attach all gems to the same side of the chain.

7. Attach one rondelle ruby gem onto the last link of the 2" (5.1cm) cable chain.

PEAR BLOSSOM EARRINGS

The changes of the seasons have inspired many poems about change, cycles, time, renewal, and life. One thing I like most about new seasons is the fresh fruits and vegetables that they bring. It is almost poetic just to hear the names of the foods. They conjure up a riot of colors, fresh flavors, and scents, and bring about nostalgic memories. Spring brings bright red strawberries; smooth, sweet cherries; and fragrant golden cantaloupe. Summer bears aromatic apricots and peaches, succulent plums and nectarines; and cold, juicy watermelon. Autumn produces the ingredients we use for baking, like delicious apples, pumpkins, blueberries, and crisp pears.

I can envision autumn with a sweet, warm pear tart with a crispy crust and a scoop of cool vanilla ice cream, or just by biting into a crisp, sweet, ripe pear. The opaque, pear-shaped moonstone gems on these earrings represent the delicious pears, and the small citrine gems represent the sepals from which the flower that preceded the fruit had bloomed. These casual earrings are simple to make, and since many gems can be found in pear shapes, you can substitute many other colors of gems.

INSTRUCTIONS

1. Cut two 2" (5.1cm) lengths of the 26-gauge wire, and then make two top-drilled gem loops (page TK) with the 10x6mm teardrop moonstone gems.

2. Cut the remaining 26-gauge wire into 8 pieces that are 1¼" (3.2cm) each, and make all of them into headpins.

3. Insert a citrine gem onto one of the headpins and then make a closed wrapped loop (page 153). Do this with the remaining
7 headpins and 7 citrine gems.

4. Open the loop end of an earwire and insert two citrine gems, then one of the moonstone teardrop gems, and then two more citrine rondelles and close the ear wire.

5. Repeat step 4 to make the second earring.

LEVEL
Easy

LENGTH
¹⁵⁄₁₆" (2.4cm)

TOOLS
Ruler
Wire cutters
Chain-nose pliers
Round-nose pliers

MATERIALS
14" (35.6cm) of 26-gauge 14k gold-filled
  wire (soft)
Two 10x6mm top-drilled faceted teardrop
  moonstone gems
Eight 3mm citrine rondelle gems
Two 14k gold-filled earwires

POMEGRANATE PULP NECKLACE

On its surface, pomegranate seems to be an ordinary fruit. However, upon splitting one open, a beautiful treasure of richly colored red pulpy seeds are revealed. When I saw the lush colored seeds for the first time, I knew right away that garnet gems could mimic this beauty, and I designed this necklace to do exactly that. It was after I called this necklace "pomegranate pulp" that I learned that the word "garnet" originates from the Latin word for "grain" because of its resemblance to the grains or seeds found in the pomegranate.

LEVEL
Advanced

LENGTH
16¼" (41.3cm) to 18¼" (46.4cm)
   adjustable

TOOLS
Chain-nose pliers
Round-nose pliers
Wire cutters
Ruler
Goggles (you will work with long pieces of
   wire)

MATERIALS
32" (81.3cm) of 26-gauge 14k gold-filled
   wire (soft)
Twelve 7x7mm faceted top-drilled flat
   teardrops garnet gems
27" (68.7cm) of 1.6mm 14k gold-filled flat
   cable chain
Two 4mm 14k gold-filled jump rings
One 14k gold-filled spring ring clasp
2" (5.1cm) of 4x3mm 14k gold-filled cable
   chain

INSTRUCTIONS

1. Cut a 30" (76.2cm) length of 26-gauge wire, and bend a right angle at 4" (10.2cm). Put the round-nose pliers inside the bend and pull the long piece over the wider part of the jaw and make an open loop (page 152) that is about 3mm—large enough to insert a small chain. Wrap the tail (the longer wire) around the stem (the shorter wire) three times.

2. Insert 11 of the 7x7mm garnet gems onto the stem (shorter wire) alternately with 6 stones on the bottom side and 5 on the top side. Lay them flat and make a slight curve on the stem. Make sure the stones are evenly and loosely distributed on the stem wire, as they will need a tiny bit of space for you to wrap the wire in between them. If squeezed too closely together, they can break.

3. At about ¹⁄₁₆" (2mm) past the last gem, bend the end of the stem to a right angle and make and wrapped loop, wrap the wire three times around the stem, and cut off the remaining wire. Don't worry if the gems get out of their alternate order as you make the wrapped loop, you can adjust them later. Also, be careful with the long tail wire, which is why you should wear goggles for this project.

4. Lay it flat, adjust the gems to their alternate order, adjust the curve in the wire, and use the long wire to weave it in and out between the gems.

5. Hold the stem with the gems in between your thumb and your index finger, keeping the gems flat and in order, and with the other hand grab the tail wire and wrap it over the first gem closest to the tail, making the tail snug around the stem in between the first and second gem once, wrap over the second gem, and wrap around the stem once.

6. Use the hand that is holding the gems to hold the two gems you just wrapped, and then continue wrapping in the same direction until you get to the end. Make sure you are wrapping the wire snugly around the stem. If you make the loops too loose in between the gems, you won't have space to wrap the wire in between the gems at the other end. But don't wrap too tightly, because that can damage the shape of the stem or break the gemstones.

7. When you get to the end, wrap the wire around the stem twice, lay it flat again, shape the curve and make sure the wrapped loops at each end are parallel to the flat surface.

8. Then, continue to weave your way back to the beginning. Wrap the wire around the stem twice at that end, weave your way a third time, and then wrap the wire around the stem three times. Cut any remaining wire and make the wire snug around the stem.

9. Cut the 27" (68.7cm) of 1.6mm cable chain into two pieces at 13½" (34.3cm) each and insert one of the chains into one of the wrapped loops. Open one of the 4mm jump rings, attach the two last links of the chain and the loop of the spring ring clasp, and close the jump ring.

10. Insert the second 1.6mm cable chain into the wrapped loop on the opposite end, then open a jump ring, attach the last two links of the chain and the last link of the 2" (5.1cm) 4x3mm cable chain, and close the jump ring.

11. Use the remaining 2"(5.1cm) of 26-gauge wire and the remaining garnet gem to make a top-drilled gem link (page 154) with an open loop and attach it to the end of the 4x3mm cable chain.

ORANGE PULP BRACELET

Slicing open a piece of fruit or vegetable can reveal amazing internal patterns. When I'm preparing food, I like to cut vegetables into thin slices and hold them up to the light to see their fascinating patterns. You will be surprised by the wonderful designs you can discover. Many resemble motifs that have been used throughout history by people from many cultures. The pattern seen in a sliced orange is similar to that of the petals of a flower. Carnelian, with its waxy luster and cheerful color, is the ideal gem to replicate the pulp of a juicy orange. You can make this same design with lemony citrine to represent a mouth-watering and juicy lemon, or peridot if you prefer light green and the tart flavor of lime.

LEVEL
Intermediate

LENGTH
7" (17.9cm)

TOOLS
Ruler

Wire cutters

Chain-nose pliers

Flat-nose pliers

Round-nose pliers

Goggles

MATERIALS
10" (25.5cm) of 26-gauge gold-filled wire (soft)

Eight 9x7mm faceted, top-drilled oval carnelian gems

25" (63.5cm) of 4x3mm 14k gold-filled cable chain

Eight 7mm gold-filled jump rings

Eight 4mm gold-filled jump rings

One filigree 14k gold-filled, 4-strand rectangle box clasp

INSTRUCTIONS

1. Making the shape of the sliced orange is similar to making a top-drilled gem loop (page 154) with 8 gems instead of one. Insert the 8 carnelian gems onto the 10" (25.4cm) of 24-gauge wire so that they are adjacent to each other and about ½" (1.3cm) from the end of one side of the wire. Then, with your fingers on the wire next to the outer gems, gently bring the ends of the wires together until the gems form the shape of a circle, and then cross the wire into an X, as shown in figure 1.

2. Hold the gems with one hand and use the tip of the flat-nose pliers to twist the wire above the X twice. Make sure the stones are evenly and loosely distributed on the stem wire before you twist the wire. Don't squeeze them in too tight against each other as this can cause them to break and they will need a tiny bit of space for you to wrap the wire in between them.

3. Use the chain-nose pliers to pull the short wire towards the inside of the circle and weave it in and out between the gems and around the stem until the wire ends. Then, make it snug around the stem. Use the long wire to do the same going in the opposite direction until it ends, and then make it snug around the stem.

4. Cut the 25" (63.5cm) of 4x3mm cable chain to 4 pieces that are each 3" (7.6cm) in length and 4 pieces that are each 2¾" (7cm) in length. Use the tip on page 157 for cutting multiple chains of the same length.

5. Open a 7mm jump ring and place it in between two gems, then attach a 3" (7.6cm) length chain, and close the jump ring. Do the same on the next two spaces and attach 2¾" (7cm) length chains, and then attach another 3" (7.6cm) chain at the fourth space between the gems. See figure 1)

6. Use the 4mm jump rings to attach the end links of the four chains to the four loops on the filigree 4-strand rectangle box clasp.

7. Repeat steps 5 and 6 on the opposite side of the orange pulp shape. Make sure to attach the 3" (7.6cm) length chains on the outsides and the 2¾" (7cm) chains on the inside connections, and attach the chains to the opposite side of the filigree clasp.

Note: If you need to make a longer bracelet, add the same number of links to each of the 8 chains.

FIGURE 1

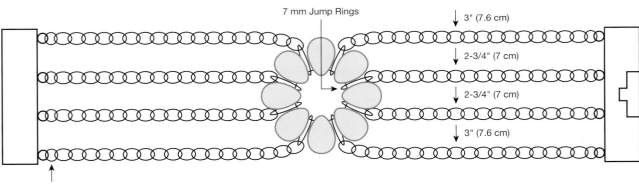

7 mm Jump Rings

3" (7.6 cm)

2-3/4" (7 cm)

2-3/4" (7 cm)

3" (7.6 cm)

4 mm Jump Rings

PEAS-IN-A-POD BRACELET

I recently bought some fresh peas in their pods at a green market. I had never bought them or seen them in this form before. As I opened them, they revealed their natural bright green color. They looked so beautiful lined up in their smooth and round shapes, that opening each one was like discovering pearls in their shells. Immediately, I knew I wanted to replicate this design in a bracelet. The soft green color of prehnite represents the peas, and the wrapped loop gem links hold them at just the right distance from each other to mimic the peas in a pod. This makes a fun spring and summer bracelet. You can easily extend the length to make a beautiful necklace and, as always, you can use any stone you prefer.

LEVEL
Easy

LENGTH
8½" (21.6cm)

TOOLS
Ruler

Wire cutters

Chain-nose pliers

Round-nose pliers

MATERIALS
22" (56cm) of 24-gauge 14k gold-filled
  wire (soft)

Eleven 6x4mm faceted flat oval center-
  drilled prehnite gems

3½" (9cm) of 20-gauge wire (soft)

Two 4mm 14k gold-filled jump rings

1½" (3.8cm) of 4x3mm 14k gold-filled flat
  cable chain

1¼" (3.2cm) of 26-gauge 14k gold-filled
  wire (soft)

One 7x5mm faceted flat teardrop top-
  drilled peridot gem

INSTRUCTIONS

1. Cut the 22" (50.9cm) of 24-gauge wire into eleven 2" (5.1cm) lengths.

2. Insert a 2" (5.1cm) wire into a 6x4mm prehnite gem and make a wrapped loop gem link with a closed wrapped loop on each side.

3. Use another 2" (5.1cm) wire and a prehnite gem to make another wrapped loop gem link with a closed loop on one end and an open loop (page 152) on the opposite end, then attach the open loop to one side of the completed wrapped loop gem link.

4. Repeat step 3 with the remaining nine 2" (5.1cm) lengths of wire and the prehnite gems.

5. Use the 3½" (9cm) of 20-gauge wire to make a hook clasp as shown on page 156.

6. Open a 4mm jump ring and insert the loop of the hook clasp and the end loop the wrapped loop gem links, and then close the jump ring.

7. Open another jump ring, insert the end of the 1½" (3.8cm) of 4x3mm cable chain and the opposite end of the wrapped loop gem links, and close the loop.

8. Use the 1¼" (3.2cm) of 26-gauge wire and the 7x5mm peridot gem and make a top-drilled loop (page 154) with an open loop, attach it to the last link of the 4x3mm chain, and then close it with a wrapped loop.

Every summer during my childhood years, my parents would pick a day to wake my sister and me up early to take a day trip. We were filled with anticipation as we would drive up to the edge of the mountains that surround the city where I grew up. As we approached the foothills, we could smell the fragrant aroma of peaches in the air. The peach colored moonstone always reminds me of those times. This bracelet goes great with the fun summer outfits you wear on hot sunny days.

INSTRUCTIONS

1. Cut the 7x6mm cable chain into two pieces that are each 2" (5.1cm) in length (8-links each).

2. Cut the 6" (15.2cm) of 24-gauge wire into three 2" (5.1cm) lengths.

3. Insert a 2" (5.1cm) wire into a center-drilled moonstone gem and make a wrapped loop gem link (page 153) with a closed wrapped loop on one side and an Open Loop on the opposite side.

4. Attach a 2" (5.1cm) length of 7x6mm cable chain to the open loop and then close it with a wrapped loop.

5. Use another 2" (5.1cm) 24-gauge wire and a center-drilled moonstone gem to make another wrapped loop gem link with a closed loop on one end and an open loop on the opposite end, then attach the open loop to the completed wrapped loop gem link on the side that is not attached to the chain.

6. Use the last 2" (5.1cm) 24-gauge wire, make the first open loop of another wrapped loop gem link, and attach it to the previous wrapped loop gem link. Insert the center-drilled moonstone, make another open loop, insert it onto the end link of the other 2" (5.1cm) length of 7x6mm chain, and then close the loop.

7. Open a jump ring and insert the last link of the 7x6mm chain from one end of the bracelet, attach the lobster claw clasp, and close the jump ring.

8. Open another jump ring, insert the last link of the 7x6mm chain from the opposite end of the bracelet, and insert the 1½" (3.8cm) piece of 4x3mm cable chain, and then close the jump ring.

9. Use the 1¾" (4.5cm) of 26-gauge wire and the 10x12cm top-drilled moonstone gem and make a top-drilled gem link (page 154) with an open loop, and insert it to the end of the 4x3mm cable chain, and close the loop.

LEVEL
Easy

LENGTH
8¼" (21cm)

TOOLS
Ruler
Wire cutters
Chain-nose pliers
Round-nose pliers

MATERIALS
4¼" (10.8cm) of 7x6mm 14k gold-filled flat cable chain

6" (15.2cm) of 24-gauge 14k gold-filled wire (soft)

Three 12x9mm faceted, flat oval center-drilled peach moonstone gems

One 14k gold-filled lobster claw clasp

1½" (3.8cm) of 4x3mm 14k gold-filled flat cable chain

1¾" (4.5cm) of 26-gauge 14k gold-filled wire (soft)

One 10x12cm faceted flat teardrop top-drilled peach moonstone gem

Two 4mm 14k gold-filled jump rings

CHAPTER NINE

EARTH AND SKY JEWELRY DESIGNS

ECLIPSE NECKLACE

On a cool, clear night, I joined friends to watch a full lunar eclipse, and someone had brought a telescope. I saw the moon in a way I never had before; it appeared to be so close and three-dimensional. The experience aroused my curiosity about the moon, and so I decided to research eclipses, since I have yet to witness a full solar eclipse. The images of solar eclipses appear to be of a perfect dark circle surrounded by glowing beams of sunlight. This glow is re-created using sparkling rondelle gems wrapped in golden wire to make a lovely circular pendant.

LEVEL
Advanced

LENGTH
16" (40.7cm) to 18" (45.8cm) adjustable; pendant: 1¼" (3.2cm) in diameter

TOOLS
Ruler

Wire cutters

Chain-nose pliers

Round-nose pliers

Ring mandrel

Goggles

MATERIALS
5" (12.7cm) of 20-gauge 14k gold-filled wire (hard)

53¼" (135.3cm) of 26-gauge 14k gold-filled wire (soft)

Ninety-two 3mm faceted, rondelle amethyst gems (amount may vary slightly)

15½" (39.4cm) of 1.6mm 14k gold-filled flat cable chain

2" (5.1cm) of 4x3mm 14k gold-filled flat cable chain

Two 4mm 14k gold-filled jump rings

One 14k gold-filled spring ring clasp

INSTRUCTIONS

1. Use the 5" (12.7cm) of 20-gauge hard wire and wrap it around the thickest part of the mandrel or any round item that is about 3" (7.6cm) in circumference or 1" (2.5cm) in diameter. Hold the wire with your fingers, making sure it is snug around the mandrel, and cross the ends of the wire so they make an X with one wire extending ¼" (7mm). Then, use the tip of the flat-nose pliers to twist it two and a half times. Trim, make it snug, and then make a wrapped loop with the longer end. The loop will be the bail of the pendant, so it must be perpendicular to the circle.

2. Cut a 1¼" (3.2cm) length of the 26-gauge wire and put it aside. With the remaining 52" (132.1cm) wire, bend the shape of a V at ⅜" (1cm) and hook the V onto the stem of the wrapped loop. Wrap the small tail around the stem and make it snug, then wrap the long wire around the eclipse loop once. This is a long wire to work with, so be sure to handle it carefully so it doesn't bend, and remember to wear your goggles.

3. Insert three 3mm amethyst gems onto the long wire and slide them down to the 20-gauge wire that forms the circular shape of the eclipse. Hold the 3 rondelle gems with your fingers so the gems remain on the outside of the circle and are balanced on top of the 20-gauge circular base wire. Then, wrap the wire around the base wire once, moving in the direction away from the wrapped loop.

4. Repeat step 3 until you reach the end of the circle next to the wrapped loop. Make sure to wrap tightly so the gems stay in their position on the top and outside of the circular ring. When you get to the end of the circle, if there is still a

little bit of space but you feel there is not enough space for 3 more rondelle gems, do not try to force them in.

5. Use the remaining wire to go back and wrap it once in between each set of rondelle gems and around the base wire, and continue until you reach the wrapped loop. This will make the gems secure so they keep their shape.

6. When you reach the wrapped loop, wrap the wire around the base once next to the wrapped loop. Then wrap it once *loosely* around the base wire on the opposite side of the wrapped loop, wrap it once more inside the loosely wrapped wire, and then, holding the pendant, pull the wire with the tip of the chain-nose pliers so it's tight. Wrap it around twice, cut off the remaining wire, and make it snug.

7. Pull the 15½" (39.4cm) 1.6mm cable chain through the wrapped loop bail on the pendant. Open a 4mm jump ring, insert the last link of the 1.6mm chain and the loop of the spring ring clasp, and close the jump ring.

8. Open another jump ring, connect the other end link of the 1.6mm chain to the end link of the 2" (5.1cm) 4x3mm flat cable chain, and then close the jump ring.

9. Use the remaining 1¼" (3.2cm) 26 gauge wire to make a headpin. Add an amethyst rondelle gem, make an open loop, attach it to the end of the 2" (5.1cm) 4x3mm chain, and close the wrapped loop.

VOLCANO EARRINGS

A volcano is often used to symbolize the origins of gemstones—molten rock that is spewed from deep below the earth. The golden chains of these earrings represent the bright, flaming lava and the labradorite with its "schiller" effect—a rich play of iridescent colors—represents the volcanic earth.

LEVEL
Easy

LENGTH
1⅝" (4.1cm)

TOOLS
Ruler

Wire cutters

Chain-nose pliers

Round-nose pliers

MATERIALS
4" (10.2cm) of 26-gauge 14k gold-filled
wire (soft)

Two 15x9mm labradorite top-drilled
faceted teardrop gems (approximate size)

6½" (1.5cm) of 1.6mm 14k gold-filled flat
cable chain

Two 14k gold-filled earwires

INSTRUCTIONS

1. Cut the 4" (10.2cm) of 26-gauge wire in half and then make a top-drilled gem loop (page 154) on each of the labradorite gems.

2. Cut the 1.6mm flat cable chain as follows: two pieces at 1¼" (31mm), two pieces at 1" (25mm), and two pieces at ¾" (19mm).

3. Open the loop end of the earwire with the chain-nose pliers and insert the gem; then insert one of each of the three different size pieces of chain starting with the longest—the 1¼" (3.1cm), then the 1" (2.5cm), and finally the smallest ¾" (1.9cm); and then close the earwire.

4. Repeat step 3 for the second earring.

What better gem to represent our galaxy than rainbow moonstone? The Milky Way exhibits light that flashes in all the colors of the spectrum. Rainbow moonstone, with its milky opalescence and sheen, represents these mysterious lights that shimmer in the night sky. This design may appear complex, but it is actually quite easy. It repeats the technique of attaching the rondelle gems on the chain links with wrapped loops. If you have the desire, you can make this design on a longer chain for a luxurious necklace.

LEVEL
Easy

LENGTH
7" (17.8cm) to 8¾" (22.3cm) adjustable

TOOLS
Ruler

Wire cutters

Chain-nose pliers

Round-nose pliers

MATERIALS
119¼" (305.6cm) of 26-gauge 14k gold-filled wire (soft)

One 7x5mm faceted tear-drop top-drilled aquamarine gem

4" (10.2cm) of 24-gauge 14k gold-filled wire (soft)

7⅝" (19.4cm) of 4x3mm 14k gold-filled flat cable chain

One 14k gold-filled spring ring clasp

Ninety-six 3.5mm faceted rondelle rainbow moonstone gems

Two 4mm 14k gold-filled jump rings

INSTRUCTIONS

1. Cut a 1¾" (4.5cm) length of the 26-gauge wire and use the 7x5mm aquamarine gem to make a top-drilled gem loop (page 154) with an open loop, then put it aside.

2. Cut a 6" (15.3cm) length from the 7⅝" (19.4cm) of 4x3mm cable chain.

3. Cut a 2" (5.1cm) length of the 24-gauge wire and use it to make the first open loop (page 152) of a wrapped-loop gem link, and attach it to the loop of the spring ring clasp, and close the wrapped loop. Insert a 3.5mm rainbow moonstone gem, make another open loop, attach it to the end link of the 6" (15.3cm) 4x3mm cable chain, and close the wrapped loop.

4. Use the other 2" (5.1cm) length of 24-gauge wire and make the first open loop of another wrapped-loop gem link, and attach it to the end link on the opposite end of the 6" (15.3cm) 4x3mm cable chain, and close the wrapped loop. Insert a 3.5mm rainbow moonstone gem, and make another open loop and then attach it to the 1½" (3.8cm) length of 4x3mm cable chain.

5. Cut the 26-gauge wire into 94 pieces that are each 1¼" (3.2cm) in length, and make them all into headpins.

6. Insert the rainbow moonstone gems onto the headpins and then make an open loop on each of them.

7. Starting on the end of the bracelet that is attached to the spring ring clasp, attach two gems to each link on the chain, one on each side of the link. Continue until you've used all the gems.

8. Insert the open loop of the aquamarine gem onto the last link of the 4x3mm chain and close it with a wrapped loop.

MORNING DEW NECKLACE

When you get up early in the morning after a foggy night and the sun is just starting to peek over the horizon, you see a magical, soft glow of light. As the sky lights up and the greens of grass, plants, and leaves on trees become visible, you can see that they are covered in tiny beads of moisture or morning dew. The gorgeous transparent green amethyst gems beautifully mimic the morning dew drops on a green leaf. This is a sophisticated and well-balanced necklace that can be worn with professional attire, for special occasions, or anytime you like.

LEVEL
Intermediate

LENGTH
16" (40.7cm) to 18" (45.8cm) adjustable

TOOLS
Ruler

Wire cutters

Chain-nose pliers

Round-nose pliers

MATERIALS
12" (30.5cm) of 1.6mm 14k gold-filled flat cable chain

3¼" (8.3cm) of 7x6mm 14k gold-filled flat cable chain (13 links)

Four 4mm 14k gold-filled jump rings

14" (35.6cm) of 26-gauge 14k gold-filled wire (soft)

Three 10mm top-drilled faceted teardrop green amethyst gems

Five 6mm top-drilled faceted teardrop green amethyst gems

One 5mm 14k gold-filled spring ring clasp

2" (5.1cm) of 4x3mm 14k gold-filled flat cable chain

INSTRUCTIONS

1. Cut the 1.6mm cable chain to two 6" (15.3cm) lengths.

2. Open a 4mm jump ring, insert one end of one of the 6" (15.3cm) 1.6mm cable chains and one end of the 7x6mm cable chain (13 links), and then close the jump ring.

3. Open another 4mm jump ring, insert the other 6" (15.3cm) length of 1.6mm cable chain, insert it to the opposite end of the 7x6mm cable chain (13 links), and then close the jump ring.

4. Cut the 14" (35.6cm) of 26-gauge wire into 8 pieces that are each 1¾" (4.5cm) in length, and use them to make an open loop (page 152) with each of the 8 top-drilled gems, so that you can attach them to the chain.

5. Attach the open loops to the 13 links of 7x6mm chain in the following order: a small gem to the 1st link; large gem to the 3rd link; small gem to the 5th link; large gem to the 7th link; small gem to the 9th link; large gem to the 11th link; and small gem to the 13th link.

6. Make sure you attach all 8 gems on the same side of the chain. There is not a top or bottom side of the chain until you attach the gems, so just make sure they all hang on the same side.

7. Open a 4mm jump ring, attach it to one of the last links of the 1.6mm cable chain and the loop of the 5mm spring ring clasp and then close the jump ring.

8. Open the last 4mm jump ring, attach to the other end of the 1.6mm chain and the last link of the 2" (5.1cm) of 4x3mm cable chain, and then close the jump ring.

9. Attach the remaining small top-drilled gem to the last link of the 2" (5.1cm) of 4x3mm cable chain.

ICICLE DROP NECKLACE

On cold winter mornings after a freezing rain, beautiful icicles can be found hanging from roofs, railings, and tree branches, creating a fantasy-like atmosphere. They capture the sunlight and sparkle and reflect all the colors of their surroundings. This beautifully cut light-pink amethyst gem reflects light like an icicle. This is a simple yet classic and elegant design that is a great first piece of jewelry for a beginner to make.

LEVEL
Easy

LENGTH
16" (40.7cm) to 18" (45.8cm) adjustable

TOOLS
Ruler

Wire cutters

Chain-nose pliers

Round-nose pliers

MATERIALS
1¾" (4.5cm) of 26-gauge gold-filled wire (soft)

One 13x9mm faceted, top-drilled briolette pink
  amethyst gem

Two 4mm 14k gold-filled jump rings

One 14k gold-filled spring ring clasp

15½" (39.4 cm) of 1.6mm 14k gold-filled flat
  cable chain

2" (5.1cm) of 4x3mm 14k gold-filled flat cable
  chain

One 1½" (3.8cm) 14k gold-filled ball headpin

One 3mm faceted rondelle pink amethyst gem

INSTRUCTIONS

1. Insert the 1¾" (4.5cm) of 26-gauge wire into the top-drilled briolette pink amethyst gem and make a top-drilled gem loop (page 154).

2. Open a 4mm jump ring, attach the loop of the spring ring clasp and an end link of the 15½" (39.4 cm) of 1.6mm flat cable chain, and then close the jump ring.

3. Thread the 1.6mm chain through the loop of the briolette amethyst gem.

4. Open another 4mm jump ring, attach the opposite end of the 15½" (39.4 cm) of 1.6mm chain and an end link of the 2" (5.1cm) of 4x3mm flat cable chain, and then close the jump ring.

5. Insert the 1½" (3.8cm) headpin into the 3mm rondelle pink amethyst gem, make an open loop (page 152), and then attach it to the last link of the 2" (5.1cm) 4x3mm flat cable chain.

MOON RING

There are different stories explaining how moonstone got its name. The most obvious explanation is its opalescent, moonlike appearance. Other sources say the stone was given its name because when you hold a moonstone gem on a clear night with a bright moon, you can clearly see the reflection of the moon in the stone, especially on a cabochon stone. In addition, moonstones are part of the feldspar group of minerals, and feldspars are actually found on the moon and in meteorites.

Most people don't think of wire for making rings. Yet it is possible to create a cocktail ring with a drilled gem where the gem appears to be set in the ring and not a drilled bead at all. This simple but elegant ring and the metallic shine of the golden wire contrast greatly with the peaceful, milky gray color of the moonstone.

LEVEL
Intermediate

SIZE
Bezel: ½" x ⁵⁄₁₆" (13cm x .8cm)—a bezel setting is a rim that holds and surrounds the gem.

TOOLS
Ruler

Wire cutters

Chain-nose pliers

Flat-nose pliers

Round-nose pliers

Mandrel

Nylon, wooden, or rawhide mallet

Goggles

MATERIALS
8" (20.4cm) of 20-gauge 14k gold-filled wire (soft)

15" (38.1cm) of 24-gauge 14k gold-filled wire (soft)

One 9x7mm faceted, center-drilled flat oval gray moonstone gem

INSTRUCTIONS

1. Use the wide part of the jaws of the round-nose pliers to hold the 8" (20.4cm) of 20 gauge wire at 3¾" (9.1cm) from one end, wrap the longer wire over the jaws, and make a wrapped loop (page 152) that is about 3mm in diameter.

2. Hold the two wires together, straighten them so they are parallel, then wrap them around the mandrel at the size of ring that you want to make. Insert the ends of the wire into the loop; hold the ring with your fingers, making sure the wire is flush all around the mandrel as you pull the ends of the wire with the flat-nose pliers; and then pull the wires back tightly to keep the shape and size you need. You can stretch the wire a bit later if you need to enlarge the ring, but you cannot make the ring size smaller.

3. Remove the ring from the mandrel, use the chain-nose pliers to wrap the parallel wires around the band of the ring next to the loop twice, cut off any remaining wire, and make the wire snug to the stem.

4. Reinsert the ring onto the mandrel and use the mallet to very lightly tap the ring around the band, first tapping it perpendicular to the mandrel to give it a good round shape, then tapping it from the tapered side of the mandrel towards the wider side to adjust the size if you want to make it a little bigger.

5. Bend a V shape at ¼" (6mm) from the end of the 15" (38.1cm) of 24-gauge wire, insert it into the loop of the ring on the side of the loop that is also V-shaped, and use the chain-nose pliers to wrap the ¼" (6mm) wire around the band of the ring, and then wrap the long tail of the wire around the same stem twice.

Note: If you use a larger gem, increase the length of this wire.

6. Insert the 9x7mm gray moonstone gem onto the wire and then wrap the wire around the band of the ring on that side.

7. Wrap the wire around the moonstone gem so it is encircled six times, wrap the wire around the band twice, cut off any remaining wire, and make the wire snug.

When I was a child, my father would take me to the mountains near our home in Japan to go fishing in the rivers. We would make a fire, cook the fish we had caught, and eat it fresh right there by the riverside. The mountain water was always cold and so clear you could see the smooth round rocks below. The river reflected the colors of the sunlight, the trees, and the beautiful flowers that grew along the river's edge. The hanging chains of this necklace imitate the sparkling river; the green and pink tourmaline stones represent the shimmering water reflecting the colors of the trees and flowers.

LEVEL
Easy

LENGTH
16¾" (42.6cm)

TOOLS
Ruler
Wire cutters
Chain-nose pliers
Round-nose pliers

MATERIALS
16" (40.7cm) of 4x3mm 14k gold-filled cable chain

Four 5x3mm top-drilled faceted teardrop pink tourmaline gems

Three 5x3mm top-drilled faceted teardrop green tourmaline gems

7½" (19cm) of 1.6mm gold-filled flat cable chain

10½" (27cm) of 26-gauge gold-filled wire (soft)

One 14k gold-filled filigree clasp

Nine 4mm 14k gold-filled jump rings

INSTRUCTIONS

1. Cut the following lengths of the 1.6mm cable chain: two ½" (13mm) lengths, two 1" (2.5cm) lengths, two 1¼" (3.2cm) lengths, and one 1½" (3.8cm) length.

2. Fold the 16" (40.7cm) 4x3mm chain exactly in half, open a 4mm jump ring, insert the center link of the 16" (40.7cm) chain and the last link of the 1½" (3.8cm) length of the 1.6mm chain, and then close the jump ring.

3. Continue to attach the 1.6mm chains that were cut in step 1 onto the 16" (40.7cm) 4x3mm chain using jump rings in the following order: ½" (13mm), 1"(2.5cm, 1¼" (3.2cm, 1½" (3.8cm), 1¼" (3.2cm), 1"(2.5cm), ½" (13mm). Before you attach each jump ring to the long 4x3mm chain, lay it on a flat surface to be sure that all the jump rings hang on the same side of the long chain and that you skip a link in between.

4. Cut the 10½" (26.7cm) of 26-gauge wire into 7 lengths that are each 1½" (3.8cm) and make an open loop (page 152) on each of the 7 top-drilled teardrop tourmaline gems, so that you can attach them to the chains.

5. Attach the tourmaline gems onto the ends of the hanging 1.6mm chains. To attach each top-drilled gem to the chain, insert the wire loop to the end link on each chain and then close it by making a wrapped loop (page 152). Remember to use the chain-nose pliers to make the wire snug.

6. Open a 4mm jump ring, insert the last link of the 16" (40.7cm) 4x3mm chain and one of the loop ends of the filigree clasp, then close the jump ring. Open the last 4mm jump ring, insert the last link on the opposite end of the 16" (40.7cm) 4x3mm chain and the opposite end loop of the filigree clasp, and then close the jump ring.

OCEAN MIST NECKLACE

On a trip to Corsica, a French island in the Mediterranean, I went on a ride in a small motorboat to a tiny island just off the coast of the main island. The sky was mostly clear blue with a few big white cottony clouds. The water all around and as far as you could see absorbed and reflected the colors of the sky in soft to deep hues of blue. Yet the water was so clear we could see schools of fish swimming below. As we rode along the edge of the island, the water splashed in silver streams of small drops that pleasantly splashed and refreshed us all and captured the colors of the sky, resembling aquamarine gems. This long necklace with cool blue aquamarine gems and the silver chains was inspired by those refreshing streams of ocean mist.

LEVEL
Easy

LENGTH
47" (119.4cm)

TOOLS
Ruler
Wire cutters
Chain-nose pliers
Round-nose pliers

MATERIALS
34" (86.5cm) of 3x2mm sterling silver
  cable chain
40" (101.7cm) of 26-gauge sterling silver
  wire (soft)
Forty-two 4mm sterling silver jump rings
Twenty 7x5mm faceted flat oval
  aquamarine gems
One sterling silver filigree clasp

INSTRUCTIONS

1. Cut the 34" (86.5 cm) of 3x2mm cable chain to 21 pieces that are each 1½" (3.8cm) in length. Use the technique on page 157 for cutting multiple chains of the same length.

2. Cut the 40" (101.7cm) of 26-gauge wire into 20 pieces that are each 2" (5.1cm) in length.

3. Use the 2" (5.1cm) wires and the 20 aquamarine gems to make 20 wrapped loop gem links (page 153) with closed wrapped loops at each end. Wrap the wire 3 times around the stem for each wrapped loop since you are using a thinner 26-gauge wire.

4. Open a 4mm jump ring, insert a loop end of the filigree clasp, then insert the last link of one of the 1½" (3.8cm) lengths of chain, and then close the jump ring.

5. Open another jump ring, insert it to the opposite end of the 1½" (3.8cm) chain, insert one of the wrapped loop gem links with the aquamarine gem, and then close the jump ring.

6. Open another jump ring, insert the opposite end of the wrapped loop gem link and another length of 1½" (3.8cm) chain, and then close the jump ring.

7. Repeat steps 5 and 6 until you've added the final piece of chain.

8. Open the last jump ring, attach the end of the chain to the loop on the filigree clasp, and then close the jump ring.

SATURN EARRINGS

In elementary school, I had to learn the names and the positions of the planets—my favorite was always Saturn. Mars was the red planet, and Pluto the tiny planet (which is no longer considered a true planet but a dwarf planet), but Saturn fascinated me most with its giant rings. There is something comforting about the shape of the circle, and these earrings with five circles surrounding a pink amethyst gem provide an intriguing yet classic look.

LEVEL
Easy

LENGTH
2" (5.1cm)

TOOLS
Ruler

Wire cutters

Round-nose pliers

Chain-nose pliers

MATERIALS
15" (38.1cm) of 26-gauge sterling silver wire (soft)

Ten 4mm faceted rondelle pink amethyst gems

3¼" (8.2cm) of 9mm ribbed round link chain (11-links)

Two sterling silver earwires

INSTRUCTIONS

1. Cut the 15" (38.1cm) of 26-gauge wire into 10 pieces that are each 1½" (3.8cm) in length, and make all of them into headpins.

2. Insert the ten headpins into the ten amethyst gems and make an open loop (page 152) on each. Use the tip of the round-nose pliers to make the loops so that you make small loops.

3. Cut the 3¼" (8.2cm) of loop chain (11-links) to two lengths that each has 5-links (cut off the center link).

4. Open the end loop on an earwire, insert a 5-link length of 9mm chain, and then close the earwire.

5. Attach the open loop of one of the amethyst gems onto the loop of the earwire and close it with a wrapped loop (page 152).

6. Attach an amethyst gem onto the each of the top 4 links of the 5-link chain. Do not attach a gem onto the bottom loop as shown in the photo, left.

7. Repeat steps 4 to 6 to make the second earring.

WATERFALL EARRINGS

Waterfalls are majestic, awe-inspiring sights whose power is both daunting and soothing. Gentle flowing waters suddenly become mighty cascades that thunderously plunge downward with rainbows of mist, and then the waters return to their soothing flow. These earrings were inspired by magnificent mountain waterfalls. The golden flowing chains depict the cascading water as it is reflected by the afternoon sunlight, and the green onyx gem represents a vibrant green pool reflecting the colors of the lush plant life nourished by the mist of the splashing river.

LEVEL
Easy

LENGTH
1⁷⁄₈" (4.8cm)

TOOLS
Chain-nose pliers
Round-nose pliers
Wire cutters
Ruler

MATERIALS
10½" (26.7cm) of 1.6mm sterling silver flat cable chains
2 sterling silver earwires
4" (10.2cm) of 26-gauge sterling silver wire (soft)
Two 4mm sterling silver jump rings
Two 7x7mm faceted green onyx teardrop gems

INSTRUCTIONS

1. Cut the chain into ten lengths that are each 1" (2.5cm) long. Use the tip on page 157 for cutting several chains of the same length. Remember that each time you cut chain, you lose one link.

2. Open a 4mm jump ring, insert 5 pieces of the 1.6mm cable chains on the first link of each chain, and then close the jump ring. Be careful not to damage the chain as you tighten the jump ring.

3. Open the loop end of the earwire, insert the jump ring with the 5 chains onto the earwire then close and secure the earwire.

4. Cut the 4" (10.2cm) of 26-gauge wire in half, and then make an open loop (page 152) on the top-drilled green onyx gem.

5. Remove two links from the third (center) chain. Then, attach the open loop of the top-drilled onyx gem by slipping it into the bottom link of the center chain. Close the wrapped loop (page 153).

6. Repeat steps 2 through 5 for the second earring.

The symmetric design of these earrings resembles the shape of a scale, like that of the constellation known as Libra. Each time you cut a chain, you "lose" a link. But those cut links can be used to make more beautiful jewelry. This design uses the opened links from other projects in this book, such as the Butterfly Necklace on page 109, which uses two closed links of chain and requires that you cut two links.

LEVEL
Intermediate

LENGTH
1⅞" (4.8cm)

TOOLS
Ruler
Wire cutters
Chain-nose pliers
Round-nose pliers

MATERIALS
Two links of 20x14mm hammered 14k
    gold-filled cable chain
Two 14k gold-filled earwires
3" (7.6cm) of 4x3mm 14k gold-filled flat
    cable chain
10½" (26.7cm) of 26-gauge 14k gold-filled
    wire (soft)
Six 7x5mm top-drilled, faceted teardrop
    London blue topaz gems
Two 4mm 14k gold-filled jump rings
Note: Natural gems often vary slightly in
size. Select larger matching gems to hang
on the center, and smaller matching gems
for the outside of the earrings.

INSTRUCTIONS

1. Cut two links of hammered 20x14mm cable chain, or use two of the links that you cut and saved from a previous project.

2. Use your round-nose pliers to hold the cable link at its center, then use the chain-nose pliers to grab an end of the wire (cable link) and pull it over the top jaw of the round-nose pliers to make the shape shown in the photo, left.

3. Use the tip of your round-nose pliers to grab the tip of the wire (cable link), curl it to make a loop and, then do the same with the other end of the wire.

4. Cut the 4x3mm cable chain to four pieces that are each ⅝" (1.6cm) in length. Be sure each piece has 5 links of chain.

5. Use your round-nose pliers to slightly open one of the end loops on the cable link wire, insert an end link of one of the ⅝" (1.6cm) five-link chains, close the loop, and do the same on the other end of the wire.

6. Open a jump ring, insert the last links of the two chains, then insert the loop of the earwire, and then close the jump ring.

7. Cut the 10½" (26.7cm) of 26 gauge wire to six 1¾" (4.5cm) lengths, and make an Open Loop on each of the six 7x5mm London blue topaz gems.

8. Attach the open loop of one of the larger gems to the center loop of the earring, then attach two smaller matching gems to the outer loops of the earring.

9. Repeat steps 2 to 8 for the second earring.

AMETRINE RAINDROPS BRACELET

Bracelets with charms are quite common. Gemstones can be used on a bracelet in place of charms. Ametrine gems, with their refreshing violet and sunny yellow sparkle, remind me of beads of water on rose petals just after an afternoon shower, when the rain clouds quickly pass and the bright sun comes out again to shine on the flowers.

LEVEL
Easy

LENGTH
8⅜" (21.2cm)

TOOLS
Ruler
Wire cutters
Round-nose pliers
Chain-nose pliers

MATERIALS
Ten links of 20x14mm 14k gold-filled
   hammered cable chain (7¼" [18.4cm])
Ten 10x7mm faceted center-drilled
   ametrine teardrops
17½" (44.5cm) of 24-gauge 14k gold-filled
   wire (soft)
One 14k gold-filled toggle and bar clasp
Two 7mm 14k gold-filled jump rings

INSTRUCTIONS

1. Cut the 24-gauge wire into 10 lengths that are each 1¾" (4.5cm), and make each of them into a headpin.

2. Insert the ametrine gems onto the headpins, then make an open loop (page 152) on each so that you can attach them to the chain.

3. Attach one gem onto one of the links of the hammered cable chain by making a wrapped loop (page 153), and then continue to attach one gem onto each of the remaining 9 links.

4. Open a 7mm jump ring, attach one of the end links of the chain and the loop of the toggle clasp and then close the jump ring.

5. Open the other 7mm jump ring, attach to it to the link on the opposite end of the chain, insert the loop of the bar clasp, and close the jump ring.

SHOOTING STAR NECKLACE

If you've ever seen a shooting star, you know the excitement it brings and the lucky feeling that you happen to have been looking up at the right spot in the sky at the very moment the star darts across with a mist of sparkles, only to quickly vanish into the night sky. It is even more exciting to see one with a close friend or loved one, which makes that short moment special and memorable. The misty gray, iridescent labradorite gems on this necklace represent the stars and the long golden chain are its sparkling path. The shooting star lariat is a versatile necklace. Unattached at the ends, this fun necklace can be worn by inserting the chain with the gems into the large links of chain on the opposite end. Or it can be tied, wrapped around the neck, or worn any other way you desire.

LEVEL

Intermediate

LENGTH

35½" (89cm)

TOOLS

Tape measure

Round-nose pliers

Chain-nose pliers

Wire cutters

MATERIALS

14" (35.7cm) of 24-gauge 14k gold-filled wire (soft)

Six 4mm round center-drilled labradorite gems

2¼" (5.7cm) of 20x14 14k gold-filled ribbed cable chain (3-links)

29¹¹⁄₁₆" (75.5cm) of 4x3mm 14k gold-filled flat cable chain

Two 13x9mm teardrop top-drilled labradorite gems (approximate size)

INSTRUCTIONS

1. Cut the 14" (35.7cm) of 24-gauge wire into 6 pieces that are each 1¾" (4.5cm) and 2 pieces that are each 1½" (3.8cm) in length.

2. Use one of the 1¾" (4.5cm) length wires to make an open loop (page 152) on one end, attach it to one end of the 29¹¹⁄₁₆" (75.5cm) cable chain and then close it by completing the wrapped loop. Insert one of the 4mm round center-drilled gems, make another open loop, attach it to one end of the three links of 20x14mm ribbed cable chain, and close the loop completing the wrapped loop gem link.

3. Use a 1½" (3.8cm) length wire and one of the 13x9mm top-drilled gems to make a top-drilled gem loop (page 154) with an open loop. Attach the loop onto the opposite end of the three links of 20x14mm cable chain and close the loop.

4. Use the other 1½" (3.8cm) length wire and 13x9mm top-drilled gem to make another top-drilled gem loop (page 154) and this time close the loop.

5. Use the 1¾" (4.5cm) length wire and a 4mm round center-drilled gem and make another wrapped-loop gem link with an open loop on one end and a closed wrapped loop on the other end. Attach the open loop to the top-drilled gem and then close it with a wrapped loop.

6. Repeat step 5 with the remaining 4mm round gems attaching them to each other until you get to the last/fourth gem, which you will leave with an open loop.

7. Attach the open loop to the end of the 29¹¹⁄₁₆" (75.5cm) cable chain and then close it with a wrapped loop.

8. To wear the Shooting Star necklace, wrap it around your neck and insert the side with the six gems into the one of the three links, leaving the end with the six gems longer than the other end.

PART FOUR

The Basics

Here you will find basic instructions you'll need

to make quality wire-wrapped jewelry.

TOOLS

Almost every piece of jewelry in this book can be made with wire cutters and three pairs of pliers: chain-nose pliers, flat-nose pliers, and round-nose pliers. Only the rings require other tools. Here is a brief description of the tools you will use to make the projects in this book and some other tools that you will find helpful.

The tools are available in a wide range of prices. The less expensive tools work just fine if you are a beginner. But as with any endeavor in which you will invest your time, you will find that higher-quality tools will make your life much easier.

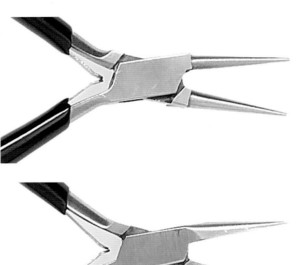

ROUND-NOSE PLIERS

Round-nose pliers have smooth, round tapered jaws. They are used for bending wire into loops, coils, or circles of different sizes. They are one of the most important tools used for wire-wrapping techniques.

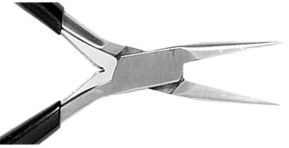

CHAIN-NOSE PLIERS

Chain-nose pliers are tapered like round-nose pliers, but they have flat, smooth, parallel jaws. They are used for holding small pieces, and bending wire to sharp angles. These pliers are useful for grabbing and reaching wire in small spaces.

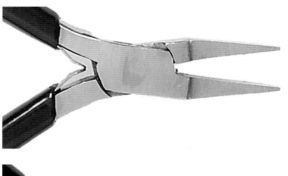

FLAT-NOSE PLIERS

Flat-nose pliers are squared off at the end and flat on the inside. They are used much like the chain-nose pliers and are good for bending wire to sharp angles or for twisting wire with their flat tip.

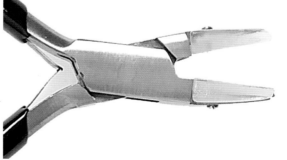

NYLON-NOSE PLIERS

Nylon-nose pliers have nylon jaws. They can be used to straighten wire without scratching it.

If you don't have nylon-nose pliers, use your chain-nose or flat-nose pliers with a soft cloth inside the jaws to straighten the wire. You can also straighten wire using a piece of leather. Fold the leather in half, use it to hold the wire between your fingers, and then pull the wire through the leather while you squeeze.

BENT-NOSE PLIERS

Bent-nose pliers are like chain-nose pliers, but their jaws are bent. They can be used like the chain-nose pliers and are especially useful in grabbing and pulling wire in hard-to-reach angles, or for wrapping wire around a stem.

WIRE CUTTERS

There are many choices for wire cutters, including side cutters, end cutters, flush cutters, and bevel cutters. I recommend the flush-cut side cutters shown in the picture. Side cutters have blades that are parallel to the handles, which make them great for cutting wire. A flush-cut means that the blades will cut the wire flat and will not leave a slant or bevel. Bevel cutters leave a tapered cut when they pinch the wire, which can be sharp and usually needs to be filed down. Flush cutters are actually designed with both a flat side and a bevel side. Use the flat side of the cutters perpendicular to the wire to get the flat cut. Wire cutters are designed to cut specific gauge ranges. Do not use them to cut steel wire or gauges of wire that are thicker than those listed on the packaging.

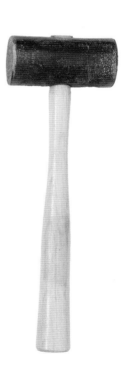

RULER OR TAPE MEASURE

You will need to measure wire, chain, and gemstones. A tape measure is helpful when using very long pieces of chain. Get something that shows both metric and imperial units of measure since many small pieces are measured in millimeters.

NYLON OR RAWHIDE MALLET

A mallet can be used to size the ring on the mandrel. A nylon, leather, or rubber mallet will not scratch or damage the wire as a metal hammer would.

RING MANDREL

A ring mandrel can be used for much more than just sizing or making rings. It can help make circle shapes of many sizes. You can find many things around the house to help shape wire into circles, but if you want to make rings at accurate sizes, it is worth investing in a metal mandrel. Plastic mandrels can lose their shape and result in inaccurate sizing.

GOGGLES

For safety, you should always wear goggles when cutting wire or chain.

FILES

Files are used to file the ends of wire, and are useful if you make your own jump rings or earwires.

SANDPAPER

Sandpaper is not typically used with wire techniques, and is more common for metalsmithing. It can be used to create a textured effect on the metal. It should only be used with the precious metals, such as sterling silver, gold, and platinum. It should not be used on gold-filled or gold-plated wire, as it can remove the layer of gold.

MATERIALS

One of the great things about working with wire is that you can manipulate it in ways that are limited only by your imagination. You can use wire and drilled gemstones to create the illusion that a gem is mounted on a ring without having to invest in all the special tools or the workshop needed for mounting gems on jewelry. Just as an artist draws lines with paint or ink, so will you use wire to make lines that connect the forms and shapes you create.

WIRE

Wire is available in many types, colors, sizes, shapes, and levels of hardness. The measure used for describing the thickness or diameter of wire in the United States is called gauge. It is important to note that the smaller the gauge number, the larger the thickness of the wire, and vice versa. The image on page 150 shows the most common gauges of wire that are used in making jewelry; it also shows the diameter of each gauge in millimeters, which is how gauge is measured in Europe.

Most of the jewelry in this book calls for 20- to 26-gauge wire. The lower gauges, meaning the thicker wires, are used for making things like rings, clasps, hooks, or findings, which need to be strong. The higher gauges are used for decorative wire wrapping and for gemstones that have small holes.

The level of softness or hardness of a wire is called the "temper" of the wire. Wire comes in different tempers, called dead-soft, half-hard, and full-hard. As the name implies, dead-soft wire is very soft and can easily be bent with your fingers. It is sometimes referred to as soft wire and is wire used for most of the projects in this book.

I use soft wire not only because it is easy to manipulate for many wire wrapping techniques and it can be easily straightened if you make a mistake, but also —and mostly—because natural gemstones are made with very small holes. The holes are small because gemstones are often sold by weight, and gem dealers try to keep as much weight on the stone.

Half-hard wire is a little stiffer than dead-soft, but it is still relatively easy to manipulate and it holds its shape well. Full-hard wire is the hardest or least malleable of jewelry wires. Although it is strong, care must be taken when bending this wire. Once it is bent, it becomes stressed at the bend, and if you restraighten and then try to bend it again, it can break. Basically, be careful not to make mistakes when using this wire.

Wire is available in different shapes. The most common is round, but wire can be found in half-round, square, triangle, twisted, and other shapes. Wire is also available in many different colors. Colored wire is usually made from copper coated with enamel. Be aware that the enamel on colored wire can be damaged with metal tools.

Wire is available in many types of metals, including the precious metals, base metals, and alloys. The precious metals include gold, silver, and platinum. Base metals include copper, brass, and nickel, and an alloy is a blend of two or more metals. Because there are so many variations of the precious and the base metals, and many terms to identify these variations, there is often confusion about what they mean. Here is a description of the most relevant of these terms.

GOLD

Gold has been one of the most valued and sought-after materials on Earth. It is the most malleable and ductile metals of all, meaning that it can be easily shaped, hammered, extended, and even drawn out, as it is in wire form. Gold is virtually indestructible. It is resistant to corrosion and will not tarnish. It has no harmful health effects and has been used in medicine and dentistry. It can even be made into thin edible foil which is used in very expensive dishes. It is reflective and has high electrical conductivity, and therefore has many uses in industrial settings. Gold is also rare, which makes it valuable.

What makes gold so desirable in jewelry is its beautiful, bright, metallic luster and its warm golden-yellow color that is an excellent counterbalance for the most beautiful of gems.

Pure gold, also known as fine gold or 24-karat gold, is too soft for jewelry-making. It is merely a 2.5 on the Moh's scale of hardness (see page 19), which is the same rating as the human fingernail. Therefore, gold is alloyed with other metals to increase its hardness.

The different combinations and amounts of metals with which gold is alloyed create various colors. Gold alloyed with even small amounts of copper and silver can make yellow gold. Mixing it with a higher amount of copper and a small amount of silver creates pink gold. A higher percentage of silver and small amounts of copper can create greenish gold. White gold is alloyed with white metals like platinum, palladium, nickel, tin, or zinc.

The purity of alloyed gold is measured in "karats," which are different from the "carats" that are used as a unit of measure for weighing gems. Sometimes, however, you will see the reference to gold karats spelled with a "c." I know this can be a bit confusing, and to make things more confusing, neither has anything to do with a carrot. Actually, the origin of both terms comes from the carob bean, which was once used as a unit of measure for weighing gems.

As mentioned earlier, 24-karat (24k) gold is 100 percent pure gold. In the form of a fraction, it is 24/24. Hence 18k gold, or 18/24, would be 75 percent (.750) pure gold. Likewise 14k is 58.3 percent (.583) pure gold, 12k is 50 percent (.500) pure gold, 10k is 41.7 percent (.417) pure gold, and 9k is 37.5 percent (.375) pure gold.

In the United States, gold must be at least 10k to be called gold. In Britain, gold must be at least 9k. Jewelers in Europe use a decimal unit in thousands to identify the purity of gold, as indicated in the amounts in parentheses above. The karat and decimal amounts describe the percentage of pure gold but do not identify the alloys.

Gold-filled is another one of the confusing terms related to gold in jewelry. Contrary to its name, it is not filled with gold but rather has a gold overlay. A layer of 14-karat gold is bonded to a base metal, or core metal as with wire, that is usually copper or brass. It is required by law to be $\frac{1}{20}$ by weight layer of karat gold. The layer makes the piece, or the wire, tarnish resistant and it will not peel or flake like gold-plated. The gold layer is usually 50 to 100 times thicker than that on gold-plated jewelry, and under normal circumstances can last a lifetime.

Gold-plated is a very thin film of gold, only a few microns, usually electroplated over a base metal. It is not a layer of gold, like in gold-filled, and it will wear quickly.

Vermeil, pronounced vehr MAY, also known as silver gilt, is gold plating on a sterling silver base. However, if the plating has not fully bonded with the silver, the silver can tarnish underneath the plating and cause darkened areas to appear over time.

Solid gold means that the gold is not hollow, but the term does not describe its purity.

SILVER

Like gold, silver has been highly valued and prized for thousands of years. It is the most reflective of all metals. This quality makes it ideal for setting off gems in jewelry. After gold, it is the most highly malleable and ductile metal. Silver also conducts heat and electricity and therefore has uses in many industries. Photography in the predigital age would not have been possible without photosensitive silver halides. Silver is an effective killer of bacteria and has many uses in medical applications. Silverware got its name from silver, as it was used for making utensils.

Like gold, pure silver is too soft for use in most jewelrymaking, so it is often alloyed with another metal. The most common alloy is sterling silver, which is made of 92.5 percent (.925) silver and 7.5 percent (.075) copper. Unlike gold, however, silver is susceptible to sulfur particles in the air, which can make it tarnish.

Unfortunately, copper also oxidizes, which makes sterling silver prone to tarnishing. This is why it is important to keep silver wire or jewelry in airtight containers so it is not exposed to air.

COPPER

Copper has been a prized metal for thousands of years, and it can have a gleaming reddish color when polished. Unfortunately, it tarnishes when exposed to air and when it is worn against the skin, it can leave a greenish cast. It is, however, easy to work with and inexpensive. Because copper wire, like other inexpensive wire, can be found in hardware stores or hobby shops, I highly recommend that beginners practice with it before they use more expensive silver or gold wire.

FINDINGS

Findings are used to put jewelry together. They include clasps, earwires, eyepins, headpins, jump rings, and various types of links, among many other components. They are available in readymade forms from many sources. These functional jewelry parts, which can sometimes go unnoticed, can be made into attractive pieces that can actually enhance the beauty of the finished piece.

The Basic Techniques chapter shows how to make some of these findings. However, it is often easier to buy certain findings, for several reasons. First, readymade findings can give your piece a professional look that doesn't have a homecrafted appearance. Second, because they are already made, they save time and trouble when making small pieces. Third, they are available in fine styles and designs that cannot be made with just wire and pliers. And finally, they are available from a wide variety of sources at affordable prices.

Clasps are used to secure necklaces and bracelets and come in all types of design shapes and sizes. The photo on page 150 shows lobster claws, spring ring clasps, bar and ring toggle clasps, filigree clasps, and box clasps. Each of these types of clasps is used in the projects in this book. Many other types exist, such as S-shaped clasps and magnetic clasps.

Earring findings also come in many shapes and styles, as shown in the photo. The projects in this book use earwires and ball and post components, which are made for pierced ears. With ear components, it is always good to use quality materials that do not cause allergic reactions, such as sterling silver and 14k gold-filled. Stay away from anything with nickel, as many people are allergic to it.

Headpins and eyepins are simple pieces that are used to hold beads or gems and attach them to other components. They are available from many sources at inexpensive prices. In the Basic Techniques chapter, I offer a do-it-yourself approach to them. The projects in this book include both readymade versions and DIY versions. The choice is always yours.

Jump rings are small rings that are used for linking jewelry pieces together. They have a break that can be opened and closed with pliers. Although you can make your own jump rings, I suggest getting readymade. Making your own requires that you either use a special blade that makes a flush cut or cut the wire with wire cutters and then file the tiny rings to make them flush. Because of all the work involved, and the risk of cutting your fingers with a file or a blade, and also because they are affordable and available from so many sources, I prefer getting readymade jump rings.

STORAGE AND SAFETY

Always keep metals in airtight containers, such as clear, resealable plastic bags. This will limit oxidation and allow you to see what is inside without having to open them. Also, remember to keep sharp tools, materials, and small jewelry pieces away from small children.

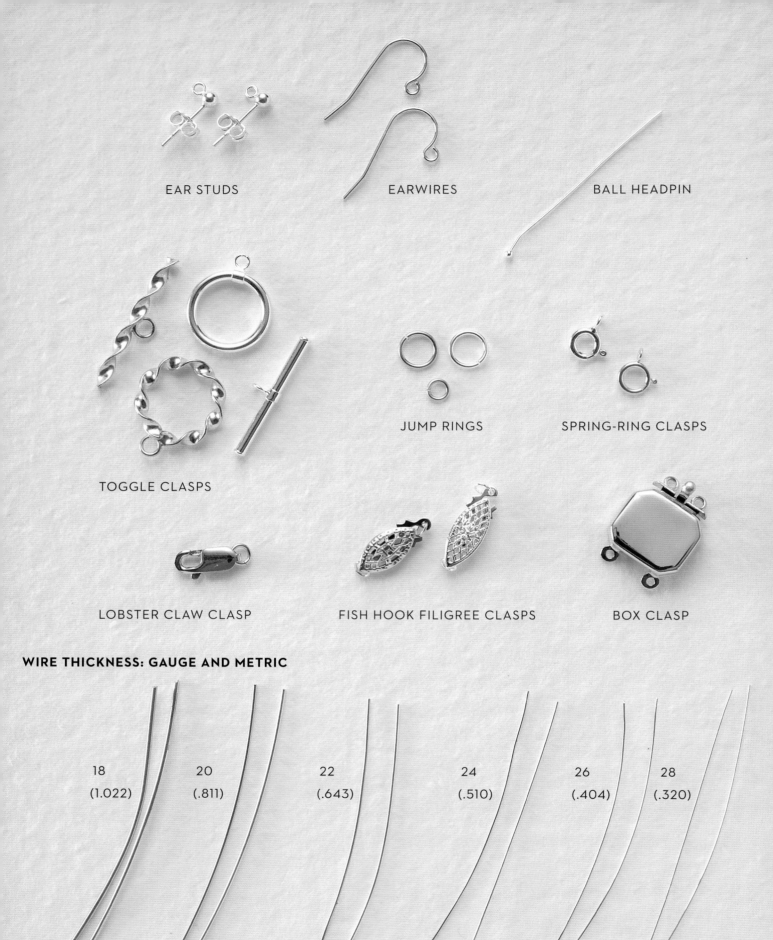

EAR STUDS

EARWIRES

BALL HEADPIN

TOGGLE CLASPS

JUMP RINGS

SPRING-RING CLASPS

LOBSTER CLAW CLASP

FISH HOOK FILIGREE CLASPS

BOX CLASP

WIRE THICKNESS: GAUGE AND METRIC

18
(1.022)

20
(.811)

22
(.643)

24
(.510)

26
(.404)

28
(.320)

BASIC TECHNIQUES

When you look at the jewelry projects in this book, you might think that they involve highly complex techniques. The opposite is true! The simple techniques in this chapter are all you need to learn to make most of the pieces. Working with wire is fun and easy. It is a bit like tying strings together, but you don't have to make any complex knots. Many of the parts for the jewelry you make are held together by coiling one wire around another, and you use very simple tools to do it. Learn these basic techniques well, and you can make unlimited designs of your own.

SAFETY FIRST

You should always wear goggles when cutting wires. You never know where the tiny tip of wire you cut off will fly. As you improve your skills, you can use one hand to cover the area you are cutting to prevent the tip of wire from flying out, but you should still wear the goggles. Also be aware that all sharp tools and materials and small objects should be kept away from small children.

HEADPINS

Headpins are simple pieces of wire used to hold beads or gems and attach them to other components. When you insert the headpin into a gem, the loop or ball at the bottom will hold the gem on the pin. Following are instructions on how to make your own headpins. The projects in this book use both readymade and homemade headpins. The choice is always yours.

INSTRUCTIONS:

Use the wire cutters to cut a piece of wire that is 11/2" (3.8cm) in length. Hold the wire in one hand and the chain-nose pliers in your other hand, and with the tip of the chain-nose pliers grab the tip of the wire and twist it to a half loop towards the wire.

Use the inside of the chain-nose or flat-nose pliers to gently press down and close the loop. If the gem or bead that the headpin is going to hold has a large hole, you can fold the squeezed loop at the end of the wire to a 90-degree angle. Most gemstones used in the projects of this book have small holes and do not require you to fold the loop.

To connect the headpin to another part of jewelry, you will need to make a loop attachment such as an eye, a simple loop, or a wrapped loop, which are described below.

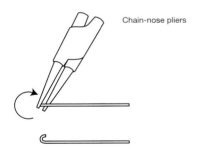

Chain-nose pliers

EYEPINS AND SIMPLE LOOPS

Eyepins are like headpins, but they have a loop at the bottom that can be used to attach other pieces. Readymade eyepins are made with a simple loop that can be easily opened and closed for attaching other parts. However, most gemstones used in the projects in this book have very small holes which require a higher gauge of wire. Remember, the higher the auge number, the smaller the thickness or diameter of the wire and vice versa. You will use a thin soft wire, and because gemstones have very small holes, I use a wrapped loop instead of the simple eyepin loop.

WRAPPED LOOP (AND OPEN LOOP)

A wrapped loop is basically a simple loop in which the wire is wrapped around the stem to make it stronger. It is used to attach components together and will be used throughout the book. The instructions are broken into two parts: making the open loop, and closing the loop. This is because for many projects, you will need to first make an open loop so that you can attach it to other components. Once you close the loop, it should not be opened again, and it can only be attached to other components that can be opened and closed, such as a jump ring, an earwire, or another open loop.

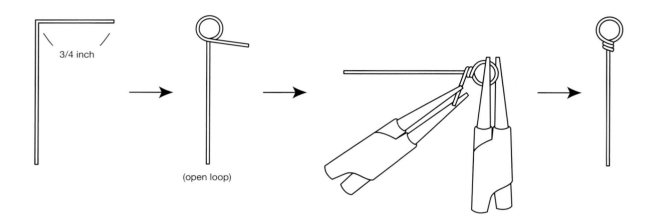

3/4 inch

(open loop)

INSTRUCTIONS:

Use the wire cutters to cut the wire to 2" (5.1cm), and then use the chain-nose pliers to bend the wire to a 90-degree angle at ¾" (1.9cm) from one end.

With the round-nose pliers, hold the wire in the bend and use your fingers to bring the tail up and over the top jaw of the pliers (the shorter side of the wire is called the tail). Position the jaws in the half loop slightly and bend the tail so it completes the full loop. You should have a loop over a right angle as shown in the above figure. You have completed the open loop.

At this point, you can hook the wire loop to other components to attach them, or you can proceed to close the loop if you are going to attach it to a component that can be opened and closed, like a jump ring.

CLOSING THE WRAPPED LOOP

1. Hold the loop you just made using the chain-nose pliers, as shown in the above figure, and use your hand or another pair of pliers (flat-nose, chain-nose, or bent-nose) to wrap the tail around the stem of the wire twice so that it forms a tight coil around the stem.

2. Use the wire cutters to cut the wire close to the stem, and then use the tip of the chain-nose pliers to press the end of the wire so that it is snug around the stem.

WRAPPED LOOP GEM LINK

The wrapped loop gem link is basically a wire connection with a wrapped loop at each end and a gemstone in the center. It is used for connecting components in the same as a jump ring, but it is stronger.

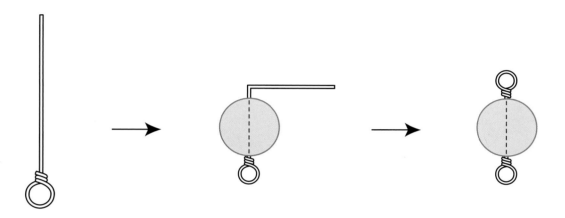

INSTRUCTIONS:

1. Use 2¼" (5.7cm) of wire and make a wrapped loop (page 152), then insert the gem onto the stem.

2. Make a wrapped loop on the other end of the wire. When you bend the wire to begin the second wrapped loop, allow enough space on the stem to complete the two wraps of wire around the stem.

Remember, you will often be connecting this wrapped loop gem link to another component, so don't close both ends unless you are instructed to, or unless you are going to connect it to another component that you can open and close.

TOP-DRILLED GEM LOOP

The headpins, eyepins, and wrapped loops described on the previous pages are used to connect gems that have a hole drilled through their center. Top-drilled gems have a hole drilled across the top of the gem, so they require a different technique for making a connection loop.

Be aware that top-drilled stones, especially those in a teardrop shape, are fragile because the hole is drilled at the smallest part of the stone, so you must handle them carefully. Most small gems have very small holes, and if you try to force a wire that is too thick, you can end up breaking the stone. If a wire doesn't fit in a gem, try another gem or a higher gauge of wire. This is one reason why these stones are sold in strands. For this sample we are using a 26-gauge wire which should fit easily in the hole of the 9mm stone.

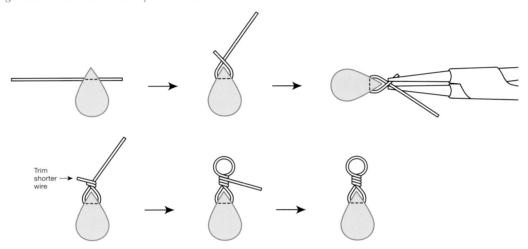

INSTRUCTIONS:

1. Insert a 2" wire into the gem, leaving one side of the wire longer than the other, approximately 1½" (4cm) for the longer side, then bend and cross the two wires into an X over the point of the gem as shown in the above figure. Make sure you leave a little space between the gem and the X.

2. Hold the gem between your index finger and your thumb in one hand and use the tip of the flat-nose pliers to hold the wire slightly above the X, as shown in the above figure, and twist the wire twice.

It is important that you hold the wire at the correct angle, or the wrap will not be evenly balanced. Also be careful not to twist the wire too tight over the gem because that can cause the gem to break.

3. Use the wire cutters to cut the short wire, and then make an open loop on the wire with the round nosed pliers (just as you did with the wrapped loop). At this point, you can attach the loop wire to a chain, or other jewelry pieces. Once you close the loop, you can only attach it to other components that can be opened.

4. To close the loop, hold the loop with the chain-nose pliers and use your fingers or a second pair of pliers to wrap the wire at least 3 times around the stem. Cut off any remaining wire close to the stem and use the tip of the chain-nose pliers to make the wire snug against the stem.

JUMP RINGS

Jump rings are small rings that are used for linking jewelry pieces together. They have a break that can be opened and closed with pliers. Although you can make your own jump rings, I suggest getting readymade. Making your own requires that you either use a special blade that makes a flush cut or cut the wire with wire cutters and then file the tiny rings to make them flush. Because of all the work involved, and the risk of cutting your fingers with a file or a blade, and because most of the wire used for the jewelry in this book is soft and not appropriate for making jump rings, I recommend getting readymade jump rings. In addition, they are also affordable and available from many sources.

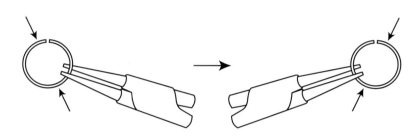 

USING JUMP RINGS

INSTRUCTIONS:

1. Hold the jump ring with two pairs of pliers. You can use two pairs of chain-nose pliers, or chain-nose pliers on one side and flat-nose or bent-nose pliers as your second pair.

2. To open the gap, keep one pair of pliers stationary and twist the other pair of pliers slightly away from you. Never stretch or pull the loop open, as this will distort the shape of the loop, making it unable to close properly (see figure above, right).

3. To close the jump ring, reverse the steps above, and to make it secure, gently apply pressure in both diagonal angles as shown in the above figure. Do not apply pressure, as in the above figure, as this, too, will distort the shape of the loop.

EARWIRES

Earwires have a loop for attaching components that can be opened and closed just like a jump ring.

INSTRUCTIONS:

1. Hold the earwire with one hand and hold the loop with chain-nose pliers.

2. To open the gap, keep your hand stationary and twist the pair of pliers slightly away from you. Just as with the jump rings, never stretch or pull the loop open as this will distort the shape of the loop, and it will not close properly.

3. To close the earwire, reverse steps 1 and 2.

HOOK CLASP

The hook clasp can be used to clasp either a necklace or a bracelet. You can easily make your own basic hook clasp.
It is like folding a wire and making a wrapped loop.

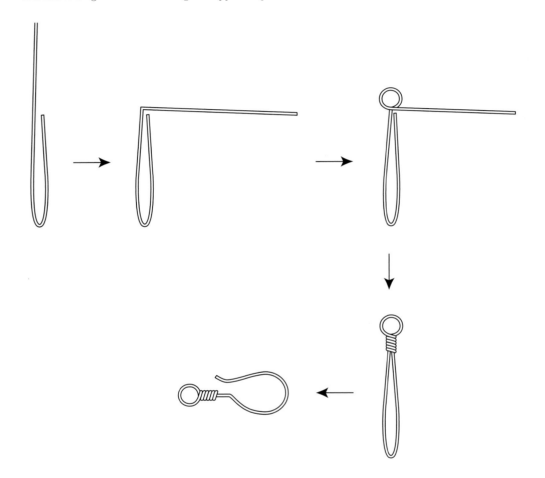

INSTRUCTIONS:

1. Cut 3½" (9cm) of 20-gauge wire (soft). Bend the wire at 1" (2.6cm) from the end using the chain-nose pliers, and then squeeze the shorter side of the bent wire is parallel with the longer side.

2. Use the chain-nose pliers again to bend the longer wire at 1" (2.6cm) from the fold making a right angle, as shown in the above figure.

3. With the round-nose pliers, hold the wire in the bend and make an open loop as shown in the above figure.

4. Hold the loop using the chain-nose pliers, and use the bent-nosed pliers to wrap the tail around the double-wire stem until the wire ends, and then use the chain-nose pliers to press the end of the wire so that it is snug around the stem.

5. Use the tip of the round-nose pliers to gently bend a slight curve on the tip of the parallel wires.

6. Position the widest part of the round-nose pliers at halfway down the parallel wires and bend the hook shape with the bent tip pointing out. Adjust the wire until it has the proper shape of the hook. See Peas-In-A-Pod Bracelet onpage 124.

CHAINS

Chains are available in many shapes and designs. It is good to spend some time looking through catalogs or at your local supplier to get familiar with the many types of chains available. Following are some tips that can be used for projects throughout the book.

CUTTING CHAINS:

Each time you cut a chain you lose one link. Because of this fact, you need to be careful when making your measurements or estimating how much chain you need for a jewelry piece. This is especially the case if the links of the chain are small or not easy to count individually. For example, you may need two pieces of chain of the exact same size. If this was a wire, you could just cut a length in half to get two pieces that were the same size. But if the number of links in a chain are even, when you cut it in half, you end up with one chain that is a link longer than the other.

Example: To cut 6" (15cm) of 7x6mm chain, each link is almost ¼" (6mm), measure the 6" (15cm) and then cut the link after the 6" (15cm) so that you don't end up with less than the 6" you need.

For this reason, when the chain is listed as a material in the jewelry projects of this book, a length of chain that is slightly longer is indicated. You should always measure the chain each time you cut it to make sure you get the size you need.

CUTTING MULTIPLE LENGTHS OF SAME SIZE:

Use this helpful technique if you need to cut several lengths of chain that are the same size.

1. Measure then cut the first piece of chain.

2. Insert a small piece of wire about 2" (5cm) in the end link of the chain you already measured and cut, then insert the end link of the uncut chain next to it.

3. Hold the wire up and cut the second chain to the exact length as the first chain. Make sure you hold the wire straight.

4. Repeat with as many chains as you need at the same length.

CUTTING LARGE LINKS OF CHAIN:

If you are cutting a chain with large links, sometimes it is easier to count the links than to measure to get precise lengths.

You can use the large links of chain you cut open as wire for making more beautiful jewelry designs. To reuse them, you must cut the link where it was welded together. This spot is usually situated where the links attach to other links. If you don't cut the wire at this spot, your piece will show the unattractive welding spot, which can also break when it is bent.

MORE CHAIN TIPS:

Never wrap chain tightly onto a spool because that can cause the links to stretch and become weak or distorted. Always wrap chain gently onto the spool.

Don't throw away small pieces of chain, as you may find a use for them in another design piece. For example, the Peacock Feather Earrings on page 108 use very small pieces of chain.

If you are using precious metals, such as 14k gold-filled, or sterling silver, do not discard the scraps, as some jewelry supplies dealers buy or accept scrap metal as credit. Keep them sorted and appropriately labeled.

SHOPPING RESOURCES

The most important thing to remember when shopping for gemstones or any jewelry materials is that it pays to shop around and compare prices. It is always best if you can visit a gemstone or supply store so that you can see and feel what you are shopping for.

The following websites have Internet directories that help you find beading stores in your area.

http://guidetobeadwork.com

http://www.beadshopfinder.com/

If you don't have a local shop, or if you prefer to shop online, here are some websites with lots of supplies and materials you'll need. This is just a sample; there are many more.

www.artbeads.com

Gemstone Beads, Chains, Findings, Wire, Tools

www.artgemsinc.com

www.beadpalaceinc.com

www.beadshopboutique.com

www.firemountaingems.com

www.jewelrysupply.com

www.limabeads.com

www.rings-things.com

www.sapphiregarden.com

www.shipwreckbeads.com

www.sohosouthimports.com

If you like the designs in this book, and would like to see more, visit www.maiflores.com.

ACKNOWLEDGMENTS

I am grateful to the many people who helped make this book possible. I thank Potter Craft's Editorial Director, Rosemary Ngo, who stopped by my jewelry showcase and first suggested that I consider writing a book about my jewelry techniques. I thank Melissa Bonventre, who patiently guided us through the initial process and supported our ideas of a book filled with the beautiful jewelry designs inspired by nature. I am grateful to our editor, Courtney Conroy, who helped us sharpen the focus and direction of the book.

I'd like to thank our photographer Marcus Tullis, our book designer La Tricia Watford, our illustrator Frances Soohoo, and the entire team at Potter Craft who worked behind the scenes, but whose work is so essential. Thanks to Potter Craft Publisher, Lauren Shakely and to Denise Peck our technical editor. I extend special thanks to our agent and counsel, Jonathan Lyons.

Finally, I thank my business partner, coauthor, and husband, Jesse Flores who spent many sleepless nights with me working on the book while we each kept our day jobs.

INDEX